The Sarah Maguire Prize
2022

The Sarah Maguire Prize
2022

Judged by Rosalind Harvey,

Kit Fan and Kyoo Lee

poetry
translation
centre

First published in 2022
by the Poetry Translation Centre Ltd
The Albany, Douglas Way, London, SE8 4AG

www.poetrytranslation.org

Come, Take a Gentle Stab (Seagull Books, 2021)
Original poems © Salim Barakat, 2021
English translations © Huda J. Fakhreddine and Jayson Iwen, 2021
Reproduced by kind permission of Salim Barakat and Seagull Books.

Exhausted on the Cross (New York Review Books, 2021)
Original poems © Najwan Darwish, 2018/2021
English translations © Kareem James Abu-Zeid, 2021
Reproduced by kind permission of Najwan Darwish and New York Review Books.

Migrations: Poem, 1976–2020 (New York Review Books, 2020)
Original poem © Gloria Gervitz, 2020
English translation © Mark Schafer, 2020
Reproduced by kind permission of the Estate of Gloria Gervitz and New York Review Books.

Unexpected Vanilla (Tilted Axis Press, 2020)
Original poems © Lee Hyemi, 2020
English translations © Soje, 2020
Reproduced by kind permission of Tilted Axis Press and Moonji Publishing Co., Ltd.

The River in the Belly (Deep Vellum, 2021)
Original poems © Fiston Mwanza Mujila, 2021
English translations © J. Bret Maney, 2021
Reproduced by kind permission of Fiston Mwanza Mujila and Deep Vellum.

Cargo Hold of Stars: Coolitude (Seagull Books, 2021)
Original poems © Khal Torabully, 1992
English translations © Nancy Naomi Carlson, 2021
Reproduced by kind permission of Khal Torabully and Seagull Books.

ISBN: 978-1-7398948-2-5

A catalogue record for this book is available from the British Library

Typeset in Minion / Adobe Arabic / Source Han Serif K
by Poetry Translation Centre Ltd / WorldAccent Ltd

Editors: Erica Hesketh and Cornelius Gibbons
Cover Design: Kit Humphrey
Printed in the UK by T.J. International

The PTC is supported using public funding by
Arts Council England

Contents

Introduction	7
Come, Take a Gentle Stab by Salim Barakat	17
Come, Dinoka Breva, Take a Gentle Stab! (Excerpt)	20
Union of Lineages	34
Exhausted on the Cross by Najwan Darwish	39
In Shatila	42
Elegy for a Sleeping Child	44
Exhausted on the Cross	46
The Sea	48
Sometimes I Wake	50
A Poem by a Soldier in Disguise	52
In Constantinople	54
My Defeated Banner	56
Migrations: Poem, 1976–2020 by Gloria Gervitz	59
From *Migrations*	62
Unexpected Vanilla by Lee Hyemi	85
World of Breaths	88
The Cupboard with Strawberry Jam	90
Taste of Flour	92
Unexpected Vanilla	94
Trace	96
Summer, When I Dreamt of Vines	98
Lalala, Cherries	100
Femdom	102
The River in the Belly by Fiston Mwanza Mujila	105
Selected Solitudes from *The River in the Belly*	108
Cargo Hold of Stars: Coolitude by Khal Torabully	127
From *Cargo Hold of Stars: Coolitude*	130
Notes on the contributors	150
About the Poetry Translation Centre and the Sarah Maguire Prize	156

Introduction

The Sarah Maguire Prize, now a vital part of the landscape of UK translation awards that recognise both author and translator, is in its second year. Created after Sarah's death in 2017 as a way to honour her legacy both as a poet-translator and as the founder of the Poetry Translation Centre, the Prize aims to recognise and celebrate the best book of poetry translated into English from a living poet from Africa, Asia, Latin America or the Middle East. The books can be published anywhere in the world and the winning collection receives a prize of £3,000, shared equally between poet and translator (or translators).

Like many people, I turned to poetry in the pandemic and read more of it than ever before, even before being asked to chair the panel of judges for this prize. It felt like the only medium adequate to contain or respond to the new or increased feelings of uncertainty, loss, anger and adriftness on a grand scale that Covid brought with it, and to provide a space where questioning, questing, is as important (if not more so) than finding any answers in what we read. Poetry affords us a vital space to sit within and contemplate both the world of the poem and the world at large, as well as our place in it. Poetry in translation does this in perhaps an even more vivid, powerful way, as we are invited to contemplate the words on the page while simultaneously imagining the words they have come from (to see or hear them through the translator's words) and the intricate mediation process that has taken place.

There are plenty of prizes for poetry that many of our shortlisted titles will also be eligible for (indeed, in some cases have already won or been shortlisted for) and this recognition is crucial for the poets involved, giving them visibility in a crowded market where it can be hard for poetry, let alone poetry in translation, to push through. Any prize that recognises both poet and translator, though, goes one step further, acknowledging the deep, careful (and often collaborative, with poet, translator and editor shaping the poems into their new English form) work that goes on to make a translated collection, and making translators visible as creative practitioners, bolstering their status as writers and innovators in a literary environment alongside the poets whose work they translate.

This year, the Sarah Maguire Prize received 55 submissions in total, representing 29 countries of origin and 15 languages, and there were 29 male poets and 26 female. Kyoo Lee, Kit Fan and I have, after much discussion, put together a shortlist featuring four men, two women, six countries, and four languages – although in

many cases, describing the shortlisted books as being translated from one discrete language does not do justice to the playful multilingual aspects of the originals' poetics.

What makes for a good poem in translation is hard to define, and there are two elements to the task we had: one, what makes for a good poem, and two, what makes for a good translation. The subjective nature of both these questions is clearly part of what makes this task hard, but also perhaps what makes it so beautifully rewarding. In our early judging meetings, the three of us naturally discussed what our criteria might be and were able to isolate a few aspects that we would aim to bear in mind while reading. These were:

- Linguistic inventiveness (or 'gingering up' the English language, as Sarah Maguire put it);
- Playfulness, or pleasure – it seemed all the more important, after the many worrying, isolating months since March 2020, to get a sense that the poet was having fun and inviting her readers to do the same;
- Collections where the reader is ushered into a whole new world with its own internal logic; poetry that allows us to 'learn a new language', or that shows us a new way of seeing the existing world;
- Collections that open up a voice that English readers are less exposed to and thus have been missing out on;
- Poetry that seemed to speak louder or more directly in the current context of the continuing pandemic, and also the war in Ukraine, which broke out early on in our judging process. Living at the same time as both these ongoing, traumatic events, we felt we wanted to read poetry that seemed necessary as a way of seeing or living or coping right now;
- Generational support – we talked about lifting up relatively new voices, as opposed to, or alongside, more established voices.

Ultimately, though, all our carefully considered criteria aside, it became clear that, as my fellow judges quite rightly pointed out, a poet or a poem could do all of the above, but if the poem didn't speak to us or 'work' in some way on its own terms, then any criteria it fulfilled would be meaningless. We all felt certain that we wanted the poetry we read to move us, and each of the shortlisted collections did just that, while also ticking some if not all the boxes on the list above.

Salim Barakat's *Come, Take a Gentle Stab*, translated by Huda J. Fakhreddine and Jayson Iwen, gives English-speaking readers the chance to explore a wide selection of this Kurdish-Syrian poet's work for the first time. Barakat writes in

Arabic, a language which has served to oppress his people but which he turns to his advantage, reminding us that it is often those who come to (a) language aslant, whether they be children, non-native speakers or those who speak a colonising tongue, who are best placed to bend it to their will in astonishing, necessary ways. The collection pushes linguistic boundaries and, while at times oblique (Kyoo Lee commented that as a reader, you 'swim through the language, but not swimmingly'), is also playful and evasive, fulfilling what we felt to be both Sarah's and our criteria for poetry in translation. The poems in translation often leave the reader with work to do – lines such as 'Don't say / sweetness is your whip with which you herd the vegetable horses, / and that the day is a goose that wandered from your iron enclosure' (from 'Fog Composed Like a Gentleman') stubbornly resist interpretation – but in this way, they re-create the original's preoccupation with the necessity and concurrent impossibility of language to depict reality or give us easy, if any, answers.

In the excerpt from the long poem 'Syria', meanwhile, the imagery is less oblique, with a strong narrative of trauma and displacement:

> Don't ask me to master discipline to master precision from now on.
> The stupefied heights have torn their vests, and the stupefied
> lowlands, like the stupid expanse, are useless, from now on.
> My knees gave out, the sky gave out.

This is a poet deeply concerned with subverting expectations of language: at the end of the collection *With the Same Traps, with the Foxes that Ride the Winds* the poet includes a footnote-like 'Vocabulary', a kind of glossary to the poems but one which merely layers confusion on top of the words it purports to define:

> Day: anger masked in air
> Wind: the steps of a word towards its secret
> Sound: the ruin of form
> Longing: gold scattered on the velvet of the end

The stretching of the limits of language here rewards close reading and re-reading, and yet there is also clear resistance, even humour. The last lines of 'Homo Erectus', the poem that closes the collection, reads:

> You have bequeathed to the descendants their desires in spoonfuls
> between their teeth. Hunters and peddlers of wounds, thieves who
> steal from death his door keys, his tobacco and the final pages of
> his account book.

While Barakat asks us to call into question language itself, this request necessarily comes from his own innovative wrangling with Arabic, in turn innovatively wrangled for us into English by Fakhreddine and Iwen.

In his foreword to Najwan Darwish's *Exhausted on the Cross*, translated by Kareem James Abu-Zeid, Raúl Zurita uses the phrase 'desperate hope', and all the judges agreed that this phrase might act as a sort of watchword to bear in mind as we read and re-read this collection. Yes, it is despairing at times, inevitably in a collection that takes us to Shatila refugee camp and repeatedly looks exhaustion right in the eye, and yet Darwish's writing manages to oscillate between showing us that despair and showing us the hope that exists on the other side of it.

In the last stanza of 'To Abdel Amir Jaras', a poem with an undeniable tone of sorrow – 'What has time produced? What have the tyrants done with / the earth? / And this river of women dressed in black, / where does it flow to?' – the poet addresses the poem's dedicatee: 'your notebook's a bird / flapping its wings in these shuttered rooms, / so come, / let me share the lack of air with you,'; despite being trapped, the bird is still alive, and there remains an impulse to share; even 'the hope that slinks off' is still moving, animal-like and devious. Darwish frequently performs a kind of demystifying, a de-clawing of death and despair, as in 'I know you':

> Despair, I know you,
> And I can hear your footsteps
> And the rustling of your dress
> As you come down the stairs.

Despair here is a romantic partner, or a house guest, something domestic and familiar, an 'age-old neighbour' the poet almost wishes to greet, although this image also reminds us of the constant proximity of such a difficult, draining feeling. In its direct, stripped-back lines, the collection demonstrates both the limits and the necessity of language, inviting us to ask, together, how we can move through and beyond suffering.

Gloria Gervitz's *Migrations: Poem, 1976–2020*, translated by Mark Schafer, is a single poem written over the course of 44 years. In free verse that drives forward like an incantation and circles back to repeated themes and images – female sexuality, migration, religion – *Migrations* performs the astonishing feat of making time both speed up and slow down at once. The effect is like watching sped-up footage of clouds scudding across a sky – the vastness of time, both in its slowed-down immensity and in its sped-up minuteness, vertiginous yet calm-inducing in its sweeping expanse.

At times the shorter fragments that sit alone on a page recall the Argentinian poet Alejandra Pizarnik's minimal utterances:

> and what will remain
> of all of this?

And:

> no one's here?
>
> no one?
>
> not even me?

In other places, meanwhile, the poem becomes multitudinous and polyphonic: reflecting the poem's travels through the memories of Jewish women emigrants from Eastern Europe via modern-day Mexican markets there are many generations, many languages (Spanish, Hebrew, Nahuatl, Yiddish, Greek, Portuguese, etc.), many voices and places jostling for space here:

> I say Kaddish for you and for me
> the words are worn like the marble of those pietás worn by kisses
> Mother of God pray for us
>
> and she who came from Kiev
> a bunch of flowers clasped to her bosom
> […]
> now and at the our of our death
> *Adonai Eloheinu Adonai Echad*
> […]
> and who cares about these memories?
>
> she a girl with flowers
> and her pleated dresses and her bright red mouth smiling
> now just a photograph stored in a cigar box […]

The migrations Gervitz speaks of are historical, spiritual and personal: movements across continents, religions and phases of maturity and, taken as a whole, act as a soothing, grounding force due to the vast perspective the collection provides.

In a lush translation by Soje, *Unexpected Vanilla* introduces us to Lee Hyemi, a young queer poet who, at 18, became the youngest winner of the JoongAng Literary Newcomer's Prize since 1963, and this collection brims with youthful, queer energy. During our discussions, Kit described it as a 'very sexy, naughty' book, and one that Sarah Maguire would have loved for its eroticism. These are thirst-quenching poems, with fluids and liquids featuring heavily, and reading them in the midst of an impending climate catastrophe and global lockdowns, when touching another human being was often impossible, felt like a balm.

A question is asked – what is inside, and what is out? Where do we end and others – or the world around us – begin? In 'A Poppy's Summer', the voice in the poem tells us they 'buried [their] ankles in the flowerbed', and 'unripened buds festered, trapped inside themselves When I opened the trickling roots and rotting taproots to draw out the fluids of sleep, sharp hairs burrowed inward'. Borders between people – between their skin, their bodies, their individuality– are rendered fuzzy and passable, as well as the borders between us as people and the natural world around us. In 'Half the Blood,' the speaker in the poem announces:

> When I stroke my cheek with one hand
> and erase my forehead with the other
>
> the evening bleeds out

They go on to compare this to:

> the sun collapsing with its face on the water
> blurring the boundaries of the world.

The fluid eroticism here creates an effect of walking through bodies-as-landscapes, close-ups magnifying skin, hairs, pores, orifices, fluids, teeth and cells. There is a joy at this melding, this blending of bodies with earth and bodies with each other, as expressed in 'Lalala, Cherries', where the lines 'Shall we fill our mouths with cherries and kiss naughtily knottily all night long' vaguely recall the meme 'what if we kissed in the [insert unlikely, or possibly dangerous/inappropriate, place to kiss]' in its playful modernity, as well as its knowingly cringe aesthetic. These poems are joyously horny, and as I write this introduction on the hottest day of the year ever recorded in the UK, the invitation to join them in all their liquid vulnerability is stronger than ever.

Fiston Mwanza Mujila's *The River in the Belly*, translated by J. Bret Maney, adds an African voice to the well-sailed course of river poetry such as Alice Oswald's *Dart* or Ted Hughes' *River*. Marked by multilingualism (there is Swahili, Lingala, Portuguese and German in here, too) and linguistic and formal inventiveness, the

collection is at once mournful, anarchic and joyous and aims, as the translator notes, to 'reinitiate the Congo River in the imaginary of European languages.' The book is made up of 101 'solitudes' which lead us through places as diverse as Minsk, Seville and Zambia, while remaining very much centred on the Democratic Republic of Congo and its rivers. Some solitudes are short, almost aphorisms, and surreal:

SOLITUDE 28

> my teeth dance the polka
> from too much chomping on my own flesh

Others are prose poems several pages long, short story-like in their detailed characterisation, but in all there is a tight control, a powerful sense of geography, and often a messy grossness – of the world and of the human bodies and minds in it. Descriptions of the river as 'a restless, twitchy dog', a 'confounded malingerer', and a water course that has 'eaten then aborted' so many of 'our own' speak to the poet's disjunctured relationship to it, perhaps a result of his being a diasporic African writer, and yet still it is inseparable from who he is:

SOLITUDE 48

> in profile, my head is shaped like Africa; if you watch closely,
> you'll see the Congo River flow out my windows and back into my
> mouth…

Along with the forced displacement articulated in Barakat, Darwish and Torabully, and the historical migration gestured to in Gervitz's work, the diasporic experience here is expressed via an attentive unpicking of the traumas and disquiet involved in global movements of people, with regular irruptions of earthy humour.

Described as an 'ode to the forgotten voyage of a forgotten people', *Cargo Hold of Stars: Coolitude* by Khal Torabully, translated by Nancy Naomi Carlson, reformulates the story of the indentured workers brought to Mauritius and other European colonies from India and China. The subtitle of the collection, *Coolitude*, is Torabully's reclaiming of 'coolie,' a derogatory word to describe these workers, and his use of it is emblematic of the linguistic innovation that fizzes across the book and functions as a sort of call-to-arms, to look to the future of migrant workers everywhere via innovation and transformation.

The collection heartily ticked the judges' boxes of 'poetry that ushers its readers into a whole new world' and 'allows them to learn a new language', this

language being what Torabully has called 'New French' – French with Mauritian Creole, Hindi, wordplay and neologisms woven throughout and beautifully brought into English by Carlson. Even without the glossary and translator's notes in the back, endless sonic pleasures offer themselves up, as in the following lines (in which the maritime terminology is just as likely to be new to readers as the Creole words):

> tack upwind
> yield to the tailwind
> keep an eye on the abacus cleat
> *babouji* broke the rope
> lookout on the port side … no
> *basbourdis guili guili oui*
> and all the sails will flap:
> 'You shouldn't cheat the sea.'

At times the speaker in the poems becomes a ship or the ocean or coastline these workers have traversed:

> My muddy future is fully abulic:
> soursop sops my flat-ribbed coast.
> You are wrong, abolished by flesh,
> your creeks crack when cutters approach:
> *tour abolie, tour à Bali*
> my backbone of kelp is the checkmate of masts.

Reading the collection is to witness the poetic metabolization of the trauma of forced displacement into something greater, something that finds a settled home of sorts in language itself:

> *In our tongues, we're at the fertile frontier of codes […] Is this why my true mother tongue is poetry? Why my only native land is the Earth?*

The six titles on the shortlist offer a stunning range of poetic experiences, showing us how both people and poetry benefit from borders being questioned, nudged at, elided. When a poem is big enough in what it seeks to do, its voice powerful and unique enough, then there is language and ideas and emotions enough to warrant – to demand! – seepage across borders into another language, another culture, another set of minds. This seepage is not a mistake, a cause for worry (though often it elicits it), but rather the essential nature of all good literature.

Translation is about movement and possibility, and these books all invite us to explore what that movement has meant and might mean: a common theme across all six books is the movement of people, whether that be via displacement through war or indentured labour – as in Barakat, Darwish, and Torabully – or via more self-directed migrations across borders of land or of bodies – as in Gervitz, Mwanza Mujila, and Lee. It has always been important for literary cultures (and hence writers and readers) to be able to cross-pollinate and speak to each other via translation, but perhaps even more so now, when in much of the world borders and barriers are being violently enforced.

The sense that Sarah always fostered in the workshops at the PTC was one of vitality, collaborative spirit and, above all, a clear belief that left no room for doubt that this work of creating translations was necessary, and always possible. In a world full of endless stark opinions (hello, social media!) where nuance often struggles to get a word in, of endless facts and 'alternative facts', these collections invite us to uphold poetry's – and translation's – innate open-endedness, its ability to allow for possibility, for multiple answers as well as questions, a quality that allows us to navigate these still-strange times, now accompanied by this wonderfully diverse range of voices.

Rosalind Harvey
Chair of the judges, 2021

Come,
Take a
Gentle Stab

Selected
Poems

SALIM BARAKAT

TRANSLATED BY
HUDA J. FAKHREDDINE
AND JAYSON IWEN

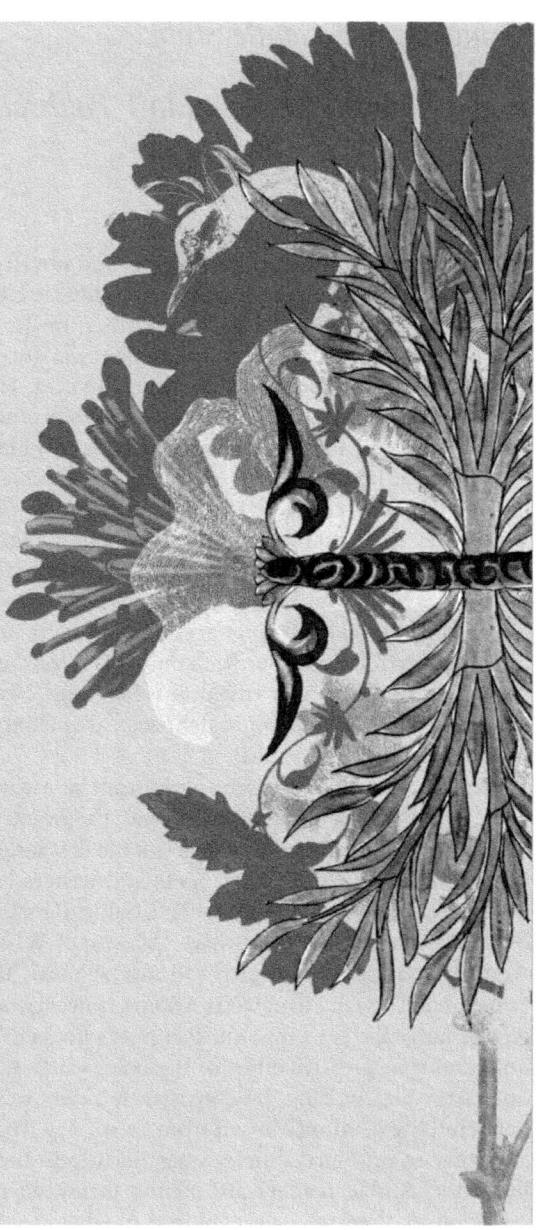

Come, Take a Gentle Stab
   By Salim Barakat
       Translated by Huda J. Fakhreddine and Jayson Iwen

Salim Barakat is a Kurdish-Syrian poet and novelist, born in 1951 in Qamishli, an ethnically, religiously and linguistically diverse city in northern Syria. He moved to Damascus in the early 1970s and then on to Beirut. In 1982, the escalating political and sectarian tensions in that war-torn city forced him to leave for Cyprus, where he remained for over 15 years. He has resided in Sweden since 1999. Barakat is often listed among the most prominent writers in Arabic. He is, in addition, the most distinctive among those included under the umbrella of writers of the 'Arabic prose poem', a term loosely equivalent to 'free verse' in English. His language is intimidatingly dense and complex, displaying a vast and daunting vocabulary. His texts are the products of an aggressive and intimate excavation of the Arabic language's creative and logical potential. He achieves the 'poetic', both in his poetry and prose, through a deliberate occlusion of meaning behind a textured and thickened language. If meaning is vision, an organizing of language into a coherent finality, Barakat's poetry is a resistance to precisely that. 'Poetry,' he states, is a 'bloody wager that drains language, like blood-letting, so it may either live or die.' It is a violent and deliberate dispelling of the comfort and familiarity we impose upon words.

Barakat insists on presenting himself as a Kurd who writes in Arabic. He is blunt in describing his relationship with the Arabic language to which he is both an insider and an outsider. Arabic is not his first language, but he defiantly plunders it and lays claim to it. Other poets and writers have validated this claim: 'Since he invaded the Arabic poetic scene, Salim Barakat has heralded a different kind of poetry' (Mahmoud Darwish); '*Mawlānā*! What have you left for us? Release Arabic poetry from your grip' (Nizar Qabbani); 'the greatest Kurd since Salah al-Din/ Saladin' (Saʻdi Yusuf). It is Adonis, however, who puts it most succinctly: 'The Arabic language is in this Kurdish poet's pocket.' These endorsements reflect the bold and transgressive ethos of Barakat's work. In *al-Taʻjīl*, collected meditations on poetry and writing, he consistently refers to the Arabs in the third person, deliberately excluding himself from them: 'My Arabic language enlists the Arab as a partner in my Kurdishness, a partnership in the heritage of imagination.' With his work, Arabic readers are on the threshold of comprehension, exceedingly conscious of themselves as explorers of what has thus far eluded them.

Barakat's work has been translated into Swedish, Spanish, Catalan, French, Kurdish and Turkish. A volume of selected poems titled *Syrie et autres poèmes*

translated into French by Antoine Jockey recently won the Max Jacob Poetry Prize. Aside from a few excerpts translated in journals and studies, this is the first book-length translation of his work into English. Our selections span his entire career thus far, from the very first poem he published in the Damascene weekly magazine *al-Tali'a* in 1971 to his 2019 collection *The Lineages of Animal*. Our selections reflect his developing craft and his ongoing interrogation of poetic language and form. Our process usually begins with a literal translation that we then work on together, back and forth, to turn it into a poetic text in English. The conversation itself, our misreadings, misunderstandings and our efforts to resolve them often reveal dimensions of the text that initially eluded us both.

Our selections include excerpts from long poems such as 'Dylana and Diram' and book-length poems such as *Syria* and *All the Doors*. In them, Barakat builds a structure from the seemingly chaotic, presenting his reader with a daunting text that requires persistence, patience and, most of all, a surrender to exultation in language. We were careful while excerpting from these texts to maintain the tension and overall arc of emotion and rhythm which holds the pieces together.

Barakat's posture towards language involves processes of uncovering, reclaiming and de-familiarising. He does not deny that it is also a difficult posture, one that does not come easy either to him or to his reader. He is nevertheless unfalteringly committed to it, although at times he does not hide his bitterness and frustration at the lack of acknowledgement by others with which his work has been received thus far:

> I don't know why I should go up the wooden stairs to the attic in one country and descend the wooden stairs into the cave of writing in another, seven days a week, in summer, winter, autumn and spring, at the same hour, and submit myself to a perilous terrifying test of the blank page and its claws [. . .]. But I know I have readers whose abilities texts cannot take lightly. They are demanding and just.

His consolation is an imagined reader, someone who is willing to follow the signs and reach beyond the easy binaries – a reader as demanding as the text Barakat performs for us.

Huda J. Fakhreddine and Jayson Iwen, from the book's introduction

مقتطفات من
دينوكا بريئًا، تعالي إلى طعنة هادئة

عندما تنحدر قطعان الذئاب من الشمال وهي تجرّ مؤخراتها فوق الثلج وتعوي فتشتعل الحظائر المقفلة، وحناجر الكلاب، أسمع حشرجة دينوكا.

(شهادة)

في حقول البطيخ الأحمر، المحيطة بالقرية، كانت السماء تتناثر كاشفة عن فراغ مسقوف بخيوط العناكب وقبعات الدَّرَك، حيث تخرج دينوكا عاريةً تسوق قطيعاً من بنات آوى إلى جهة أخرى خالية من الشظايا.

(شهادة)

دينوكا. ماذا أقول للصيّادين الذين يضعون سروجاً فوق ظهور الكلاب السلوقية في سفح سنجار وجبال عبد العزيز؟ أنت مختبئة في مكان ما، ربما في زريبة، تشمّين التراب ومزاود النعاج. كبيرة أنتِ، بليلةٌ، مسكونة بالحصاد وبي.

أسمع والدك يصيح: "دينوكا.." أسمع والدتك تصيح: "دينوكا، احملي خبز الشعير هذا إلى المهاجرين وقولي أن يستريحوا قليلاً".. كان عددهم يزداد يوماً بعد يوم.. من طشقند وخوزستان وأرمينيا والجنوب الغربي لروسيا حملوا أشرعتهم وصرر السرخس إلى الجزيرة بلا أحذية أو مناجل. وكنت صغيرة لم تدركي أنهم يحتاجون إلى الماء وإلى امرأة مجنونة أو أرملة يدفنونها بعيداً في شقوق البراري لتنبتَ في سنيّ الهجرات عَدَساً وجنادب. أنت تجهلين كيف يمتلىء الأخدود بين "عامودا" و"موسيسانا" بجثث البغال والأعضاء المبتورة. تجهلين من أين يحصل البدو على بنادق فرنسية، ولماذا ينتفخون على تخوم القرى حين يهجمون عاصبين رؤوسهم بعباءاتهم.

Come, Dinoka Breva, Take a Gentle Stab! (Excerpt)

When the packs of wolves descend from the north, dragging their asses through the snow, howling and setting the locked barns and throats of dogs ablaze, I hear Dinoka's death rattle.

In the watermelon fields around the villages, the sky used to scatter, revealing a void canopied by cobwebs and policemen's caps. Dinoka emerges naked, leading a pack of jackals in a direction empty of shrapnel.

Dinoka!

What shall I say to the hunters who saddle their hounds on the slopes of Sinjar and the mountains of Abdelaziz? You are hiding somewhere, perhaps in a barn, breathing in the earth and the mangers. You are grand and damp and haunted by the harvest and me.

I hear your father calling: 'Dinoka …' I hear your mother calling: 'Dinoka, take this barley bread to the immigrants. Tell them to rest awhile.'

There were more and more of them, day after day … from Tashkent, Khuzestan, Armenia and southwest Russia. They carried their sails and bundles of fern to the peninsula, without shoes or scythes. You were too young to realize how much they needed water; how much they needed a madwoman or a widow to bury deep in the cracks of wilderness, so she could sprout lentils and grasshoppers in the years of exodus. You didn't know how the trench between Amuda and Mosissana brims with the carcasses of mules and amputated limbs. You didn't know from where the Bedouins get French rifles, and why they swell at the edges of the village before attacking with cloaks wrapped around their heads.

قيل: خرجتِ من جهة العراء، وخرجتْ "بريثا" من جهة العراء، ومن جهة العراء خرج الله، وجاءت الدهشة والطلقات الفارغة التي جلبها الصِّبية من براميل قمامة السراي. وقيل إنكِ عدتِ بقطيع من النعاج المبتهجات وكبش واحد يخزّ كالمحارب في كل موضع مبلل بالبول.

دينوكا.. دينوكا

أنا متعب، ولا أسمع صوتك حيث أرى هضاب "معيريكا" وعربات الأكراد المحملة بالقش.

فرمان/ المطاردة

يا ابنةَ أيامي الزانية
لا بغلك، لا البريّة، لا الأسلاك تواريكِ، وطيفُك - هذا المشطورُ -
يميل وأسنده لأطيلَ مطاردتي
فأنيخي طائرَك اليوم بمنحدر خلف جنازة أغصاني
إني متّصل بالفلك الدائر، بالهمس، وظلّ المقصلة.

* * *

خلف الشجرات
كان النسّاجون يديرون على النَّول خيوطَ الهدنة بين الوحشة

It is said: You sprang forth from the direction of wilderness, and Breva sprang from there too. From the direction of wilderness, God sprang forth and from there too sprang wonder and the bullet casings children dug from the palace trash. It is said you returned with a flock of merry ewes and a single ram that heaved like a warrior over every spot wet with piss.

Dinoka … Dinoka …

I am tired. I don't hear your voice when I behold the hillsides of M'airika and the hay-heavy carts of the Kurds.

A DECREE: THE HUNT

Daughter of my whoring days.
Your mule no longer hides you, nor does the wilderness or the wires.
And your ghost, this cleft one, I will prop up when it falters, to prolong my chase.
Let your bird alight on a slope, beyond the funeral of my branches.
I am tied to the orbiting sphere, to the whispers and the shadow of the guillotine.

* * *

Beyond the trees,
on their loom, weavers have spun the threads of truce between

والعالم؛ خلف الشجرات كَبَتْ رئتي
ثم اتكأتْ فوق جذوع يابسة واشتعلت؛

أشعلتُ النساجين الفقراء فهزّوا خاصرتي وتهاووا
فوق جذوع يابسة يعتصمون بأزهاري ونباتي،
يعتصمون بقفازات امرأة تتراجع قُدَّامَ البدو المرتعبين
على فوهة أوردتي.

خلف الشجرات، قناديل الماء، غبارٌ ألمحُ فيه يديك تذوبان..
أنيخي يا ابنة أيامي الزانيةِ
لا البريّة، لا الأسلاك تواريكِ، بجانب دغلٍ أو جبلٍ سوف ترينَ معي مطري
ونهاري متّكئاً تتجاذبه الرأفة والريح وظلّ المقصلة

وترينَ عصافير دمي المتغافل
(ثمة وعدٌ أن أتجاهلها كالشرفاء
فلا آتيها بين جواري الجمهورية والحرّاس)
ترينَ دمي
محتشداً بملوك البحر وقرميد المدن
وأنا أتجاهل أقواماً يقتربون ويمضون، وأثقب نعلِيَّ لأعرف
ما يعرفه الصعلوك عن الشهداء المنبوذين على طرقات الأضرحة
ولأعرف كيف يهادنني زمني
وسهوبٌ تكتظّ بعشب يحزنني
(يحزنني البرق إذا أومض في أطراف السيل، ويحزنني السيل
إذا فاض على البرّ ويحزنني البرّ إذا أقصَتْه الدولة عن تاريخ الدولة؛
تحزنني الدولة إن قاطعها الحزن. يحزنني الحزن)

أنا خلفك يا ابنة أيامي الزانيةِ
أدعو ورق العنّاب إلى حيرة العشب: "خُفَّ إلى ضاحيتي
يا ورق العنّاب بسوريّة". عجِّل بالله، أنا مشغول بدخانٍ يعصمني
من حرية أجيال تقتنص الأجيالَ؛ مدايَ سروجٌ وعجاجٌ
أقترح اسماً آخر فيه لمائي

despair and the world. Beyond the trees, my lungs slumbered, leaning against dry trunks, and were set ablaze.

I set the poor weavers on fire. They shook me and fell clinging to my flowers and plants. They took refuge in the gloves of a woman who retreats from Bedouins trembling before my gaping veins.

Beyond the trees are water lamps and dust. Through it, I witness your hands melting …
Kneel down, daughter of my whoring days!
Neither the wilderness nor the wires can hide you now. Beside a thicket or a mountain, you and I will watch my rain fall and my day bend, tossed back and forth by benevolence, by winds and the shadow of the guillotine.

You shall see the birds of my oblivious blood
(I have vowed to ignore them, as becomes noblemen,
never to acknowledge them before the guards and slave girls of the Republic).
You shall see my blood
swamped with sea kings and city brick.
I ignore people who come and go. I pierce the soles of my shoes so I may know what a tramp knows of martyrs, abandoned on paths to the mausoleum,
so I may know how my time appeases me,
how the prairies swarm with grass that saddens me
(I am saddened by lightning when it strikes the edges of the flood; saddened by the flood when it swells ashore; saddened by the shore when banished from history by the state; saddened when sorrow deserts the state; saddened by sorrow.)

Standing behind you, Daughter of my whoring days,
I summon the jujube leaves to a people's bewilderment: 'Hurry to my suburb, O Jujube of Syria! Hurry, by God! For I am mesmerized by a smoke that holds me from the freedom of generations hunting generations. My horizon is saddles and battle dust, and by it I

وأصاحب ثدييّات العصر إلى بهو سمندله وخزاماه، إلى ثديٍ فاجأه الله وراء السنبلة.
يا ورق العنّاب، الجغرافيون نيامٌ، والطلقات مُلئنَ بأسرار العشب..
"أنا الربّان وباخرتي
صدأ الخطوات". وراءكِ، عن جنبيكِ ترينَ دمي
يبعث هاوية في هاويتي
ويهيب بسرب من أفراس الوحشة يتمطّى وسط سياجات الروحِ،
ويصهل في ثوب "بريڤا" المقتولة بالغرباء وطقس الآلهة.
أجنح للعنف وأعقد أمعاء الأفراس إلى وتدٍ يحتكّ به الشركس والكرد وينتصبون خفافاً.

أختم وارقهم بالنرجس والإيمان الأبديّ ونمضي شجراً وعصافيرَ إلى النهر،
نقول: "تعالَ أيا نهرُ،
تعالَ أيا جبلُ"
ونقول: "تعالَ أيا حجلُ
تعالَ أيا ورق العنّاب إلى باديةٍ تخرج من ثقب الجمجمة".

[. . .]

أ/
لا فاصل في ذرّاتي غير حفيف سراويل المطر الوضّاء.
—تجزّأ
—أتجزّأ،
فلتتجزّأ من حشرجتي الساحات لأفرحَ بالأعلام مع الثورة توصد عزلتها وتخاصم من يأتيها متّحداً.

suggest another name for my water. I accompany the mammals of this age to the great hall of salamander and hyacinth. I lead them to a breast that God has taken by surprise behind the wheat stalk.
O Jujube, the geographers are asleep and the bullets have been loaded with the secrets of grass.
'I am the skipper and my ship is the rusty trail.' You see my blood all about you, circling an abyss within my abyss, frightening a herd of desolation's mares stretching within the fences of the soul, neighing beneath Breva's gown as strangers and the rites of the gods slay her.
I choose vehemence and tie the entrails of the mares to a post against which the Circassians and the Kurds rub themselves and stand erect.

With Narcissus and unwavering faith, I seal their buds, and like trees and birds we head for the river,
'Come along, O river!
'Come along, O mountain!' we say.
'Come along, O partridge!
'And you, O leaves of jujube, come to the desert that spills from a crack in the skull!'

[...]

A.
There is no space in my atoms but the rustling of the bright rain's pants.
—Break down.
—I break down.
Let my death-rattle break down the squares, so I might rejoice in flags besieging the Revolution, resisting those who come together.

ب/
لا فاصل في ذرّاتي غيرُ دلال العشب.
—تجزّأ،
—أتجزّأ،
وأهدّد من يأتيني متّحداً.

ج/
لا فاصل في ذرّاتي غير جراثيم الحربِ،
تعالوا
محظياتٍ وسراديبَ وأقماراً بائسة تتدلى من أعمدة الهاتف والجوع. تعالوا ملتحمين بقصدير الضوضاء لأَقَصّلكم وأسلّمَ كل فريق فلكَ القنبلة.
إني وارثكم في النسوة، آتي الأم على مضجع ابنتها،
أو أجمع شمل الأختين على شفرة أنفاسي
وأقود شعائركم في ميناء الورد إلى زورق شحن الربّات وأيام الباب العالي مكتظّاً بأنابيق الزندقة.

د/
لا فاصل في ذرّاتي غير جذور خُراسانَ،
—تجزّأً
—لن أتجزّأ في معتَقَلٍ
أقدر أن أنفذ منه إلى الطاعون. تعالوا دسّاسينَ ولوطيينَ، تعالوا حشاشين نفاجئ أجراسي.

أصغيتُ إلى العالم
أصغيتُ إلى دينوكا يريڤا
أصغيتُ إلى سمتي ونعاسي
أصغيتُ إلى الحبّ يرندحُني في خلخلة العصيان ويفتتح السِّلم الموقوت بأهداب نساء يتكاثفن، ويهطلن على مدخنة الفقراء...

B.
There is no space in my atoms but the people's indulgence.
—Break down.
—I break down,
and I threaten those who come to me unified.

C.
There is no space in my atoms but the germs of war.
Come to me,
paramours, crypts and desolate moons dangling from hunger and
telephone poles. Come to me melted in the tin of commotion so I
may reshape you and hand each team its orbit of grenade. I am an
inheritor of your women, for I take the mother on the daughter's bed,
unite the two sisters under the blade of my breath,
and lead your rituals at the port of roses, which ship off goddesses
and the days of glory,
a boat overcrowded with alembics of blasphemy.

D.
There is no space in my atoms but the roots of Khursan.
—Break down.
—I will not break down in a detention camp
I can escape from to the plague. Come to me, schemers and sodomites.
Come, all you addicts and let us take my alarms by surprise.

I listened to the world
I listened to Dinoka Breva
I listened to my impression and my drowsiness,
I listened to a love that lulls me in the stupor of sedition, establishes
a peace timed by the eyelashes of women growing denser, women
overflowing the chimneys of the poor.

[. . .]

وغزالات ليس تترجمُ، وأترجمُها:
"كلُّ غزال فاتحةٌ"
وأترجم في الهضبات الأعلامَ: "صحونا ورأيناك شظيّة
تنقل عائلة الرمل إلى الخوذة، والعربيّ إلى ذاكرة في
صوديوم الكون؛
دعوناك باسمك،
ودعوناك باسم الماسة والمرجانة: كنتَ بلا مددٍ
وجهاتك تتراخى كالعضلات وتُرخيكَ،
وكان النمل يجمع ما يتهاوى منك على الأرض خليّة
خليّة
خليّة
وتقوم على هيئة مخلوق مرصوص بحجارة ما قبل الميلاد
وما بعد الميلاد؛
رأيناك تصيح: أنا براهماتيُّ النمل أسير به في ملكوت حدادي،
فقتلناكَ".
أبارك حنجرتي
وأزاحم في خلوات الغيم نهاري عَلَماً عَلَماً نحو سنابل دينوكا:

"ماذا يفعل مثلي إلّا أن يستفرد مثلك للقتل، وأن يتقصّى أعضاءك
بعد القتل ويخرجَ مجنوناً يطلب موتَ الإنسان وموتَ البحر
وما سوف يدبّجه المستقبل من فلِزاتٍ وأكاسيدَ لخلق أجنّته؟
ماذا أفعل وأنا خلف الشجرات..."

[. . .]

[. . .]

Untranslatable gazelles and yet I translate them:
'Each gazelle is a beginning.'
And on the hills, I translate the banners: 'We awoke to find you a
splinter conveying the sand family to the helmet, and the Arab to a
memory within the sodium of the Universe.
We called you by your name.
We called you in the name of the diamond and the pearl; helpless
you were
and like muscles your destinations slackened, and you sagged,
and ants collected what fell from you to the earth,
cell
by cell
by cell.
You rose up into a creature built of stones before Christ and after.
We saw you cry out: 'I am the Brahman of ants! I drive them into my
kingdom of lamentation where we killed you.'
Bless my throat
under the retreat of clouds, banner by banner, I hustle my day
towards Dinoka's wheat stalks:

'What does someone like me do but corner someone like you for the
slaughter. What else but examine your organs after the slaughter
and go mad, demanding the death of man and the death of sea and
the death of all metals and oxides the future might fashion to create
its foetuses?
What can I do beyond trees?

[. . .]

مَنْ أُوقِظُ في خلوات الجغرافيا بعدُ ليشهدَ لي وعليَّ ومجزرتي تستسقي من أحواضٍ في مفترق العالم والله؟

[...]

قلت غداً أمضي لغد يتراجع أو ينعطف
في زاوية قبل حدود الإنسان؛
سمعت الإنسان يرتق حاضره ويموت فهرولت إلى السنبلة
لتبلَّغ دينوكا أني قادم
ومعي بعض الأعذار على ورقٍ خشية أن أتلعثم حين ألاقيها،
ومعي هاويتي.

Whom do I call upon in the seclusions of geography, whom do I call upon to witness my massacre asking for water from pools at the intersection of the world and God?

[. . .]

I said: Tomorrow I will set out towards a tomorrow that retreats or turns
a corner before the limits of the human;
I heard the human wrap up his present and die. I rush to the wheat stalk so it may tell Dinoka I'm on my way.
I carry a few excuses scribbled down, lest I stutter when I see her, and always with me, I carry my abyss.

نقابة الأنساب

"هذا وجهي العصريُّ"
أنا آتٍ
فليرقبْ كلُّ مليك شحّاذ في أرض الردّة من أين تجيء الطعنات.
عبر تخوم الغربة في أجفان صبايا الله وعبر الساقية
أختصر الزمن الخائف في عين النسوة، أزجي الزمن القرشيَّ إليها
لا الدمعُ ولا نزف الفقراء ينيخ الرَّحْلَ، طوافي
خلف قوافل زغب.. فليرقب
كلّ مليك شحّاذ في أرض الردة من أين تجيء الطعنات.

"هذا وجهي العصريُّ"
بلا نعل أرحل نحو بلاد الفرس وأمصار الروم وأرفع وجهي
للظلمات أسائلها
وأسائل رجليَّ الداميتين عن الأرض العمياء وهمس
خفافيش سمائي
وبكل مثولي بين يد الغربة أصرخ:

تصهل أفراس الحرب على أبواب الكعبة يا أهل الشام ووحدي
أبسط للملتجئين إلى ظلّ الأحجار السوداء ردائي
أتقطّع حين ينوس الموت على وجه الحُجّاج،
وبين الصدر المشْرَع للطعنة والرمح الظّامي أتخثر،
أزحمُ ملكوتَ الرهبة صَدْعاً يفصل عربات الزمن اللاهث
قُدّامي ورائي
أتصاعد في أنفاس الكعبة جمراً تتنفّسُهُ الصحراء فتحبو
حاملةً هزجَ قبائلها نحو قوافي الحرب؛ أزنِّرُ نسب الراجل
بالفارس، والهارب
بالثابت في الحومَة حتى يرخي النخلُ النادبُ جنحَ الدمع عليَّ..

Union of Lineages

'This is my modern face.'
Here I come.
Let every little beggar king in the land of apostasy be wary of where the stabbing will come from.
At the limits of desolation in the eyes of God's waitress and maidens,
I abridge the frightened time in the female eye.
I shove the Qurayshi time to it.
Neither tears nor the blood of the poor can stop this wandering,
my roving
after caravans of fluff … Let him beware.
Let every little beggar king in the land of apostasy be wary of where the stabbing will come from.

'This is my modern face.'
Shoeless I travel towards Persia and the Byzantine capitals. I raise my face to the darkness asking, and I ask my bloodied feet about the blind land and the heavenly whispers of bats,
and standing in the palm of exile, I shall scream:

O people of Syria, the war steeds are whinnying at the gates of the Kaaba and I alone
spread my cloak for those who seek refuge in the shadow of black stone.
I am torn apart when death dangles over the pilgrims' heads.
Between the bare chest and the thirsty spear, I coalesce.
I crowd the kingdom of terror into a crack, parting the cargo of the panting time
before and behind me.
I rise in the breath of the Kaaba, a smouldering the desert exhales as it drags the clamour of its tribes towards songs of war.
I fasten the lineages of he who goes on foot and he who mounts, he who flees and he who stands his ground in the fray, until the wailing palm tree drapes a wing of tears about me . . .

أبايع في حمحمة الأرماح لوائي
أضربُ شرقاً، غرباً، ضربَ اليائس.. يسقط وجهي الأوّل
أضربُ.. يسقط وجهي الثاني
أتراجعُ بالحُجّاج إلى عرفاتَ غباراً يتكسّرُ تحت حوافر ريح الوهن القاصم
ثم نموت لنحلم
ثم نقوم لنحلم
ثم نفصّد أوردة كي نلمح في الدّمِ مجيءَ الأشجار مع اليوم التالي عاقدةً
فرحَ الأنهارِ على الهاماتِ عمائم.

In the rattle of spears, I pledge allegiance to my banner
and I strike east, west. I strike in despair … and my first face falls.
I strike …and my second face falls
I retreat the pilgrims to Arafat as dust crumbling under the hooves
of the shattering winds.
We then die, so we may dream.
We then rise, so we may dream.
We then open veins, so we may see in blood the coming of trees
with the new day,
wrapping the joy of rivers like turbans about their tops.

Najwan Darwish

Exhausted on the Cross

TRANSLATED BY KAREEM JAMES ABU-ZEID
FOREWORD BY RAÚL ZURITA

NYRB/POETS

Exhausted on the Cross
  By Najwan Darwish
    Translated by Kareem James Abu-Zeid

From *Nothing More to Lose* and *Je me lève rai un jour* (*I Will Rise One Day*) to the present collection *Exhausted on the Cross*, the multifaceted poetry of Najwan Darwish puts us again and again in front of the contours of something immemorial, almost unspeakable. It tells us that above all else poetry is solidarity and compassion for every detail of the world: for that specific bread and oil, for that eternity at the breakfast table, for that land with its 'graves by the river'. The poem 'My Defeated Banner' shows us those graves, it explicitly tells us that they are there, by the river; and for a second we see that if that image moves us, it is because – whatever our countries, origins, and histories, and even whatever languages we speak and, beyond that, whatever times we have lived and died in – we have all been buried in those graves and, at the same time, we have all wept over them.

The characters that move through the seven sections that make up this book are exhausted, exhausted in an infinity of crosses that rise in an infinity of places. Expelled from their ancestral land, permanently besieged and persecuted, women who have lost everything – their houses, their neighbourhoods, their children – make present to others, to me, to you, to the reader, that in this land of victims and perpetrators, displaced and disappeared, all the rest of us are survivors. And if we can affirm that we are facing political poetry, it is because we do it as survivors of an unfinished war. Far removed from any pathos or self-pity and, on the contrary, endowed with a stirring familiarity with everything it names, a familiarity that often resorts to irony and humour, Najwan Darwish's poetry travels through the villages, landscapes, neighbourhoods, cities, and towns of a history that is three millennia old, one that, in each of its corners, preserves the remains of a permanently shattered eternity, as if there were an underlying god, not named, who took pleasure in weaving together suffering and misfortune.

In a world of victims and victimizers, it has fallen to the poet to be the first victim to cross the land of the dead and of silence, and also to be the first to rise up and tell us that despite everything, new days will come. At ground level, then, Najwan Darwish's poems re-emerge from their own silence, signalling that nothing would exist were it not for the fact that the most imperishable aspect of the human dream is inscribed in the hope of a new day.

The question that Darwish's extraordinary poetry leaves us is: How, in the face of the endless cohort of sufferings, the thousands and thousands of refugees

who die daily in the Mediterranean, the ones kidnapped and beheaded by drug traffickers, the constant bomb ings, the hunger – how can one bear it all? Why doesn't the woman whose children were killed by a tank commit suicide? Why do those millions and millions of people who survive in indescribable conditions continue to fight for their right to life? Whatever the answer, if we add up, one by one, the reasons – almost inaudible, minimal, unthinkable – that allow the most devastated of people not to kill themselves and that lead them to choose, second after second, to remain alive, that sum would form the image of Paradise, or of a seed sprouting and budding. It's there that the sunny morning would be – the broken husband returning from his work, the rebuilt house, the milk that the mother did not have for her dying child; it's there that the bread would be, and the warmth of the bed whose mattress, still intact, peeks out from the rubble.

Raúl Zurita (translated by Frances Simán), from the book's introduction

في مخيّم شاتيلا

تَقِفُ في القَيْظِ أمامَ "بَيْتِها" في مُخيَّمِ شاتيلا
تَقولُ لَكَ العَجوزُ السّامقةُ التي خَرَجَتْ مِنْ حَيْفا وعُمْرُها تِسْعَةُ أَشْهُرٍ
وهي الآنَ في الخامِسَةِ والسِّتِّين:
"عايْشين بِذُلّ هُون"...
في كَلِمَتين
في لَحْظَتَيْن تَقولُ لَكَ كُلَّ شَيء

أنْهُرٌ مِنَ النَّدَم
سَنواتٌ طَويلةٌ مِنَ العَذاب
تَغْرَقُ في الكَلِمَتين.

تَنْظُرُ إلى ظَهْرِها المُنْحَني
وتَتَذكَّرُ أشجارَ الصَّنوبَرِ في الكَرْمِل
تَنْظُرُ إلى عَيْنَيْها
وتَتَذكَّرُ سَماحَةَ الشَّاطئ
تشكو لَكَ مِنْ ماءِ البَحْرِ المالِحِ في الحَنفيّات
ولا تستطيعُ سوى أنْ تَبْتَسِم وأنتَ تَفْتَحُ قَلْبَكَ لهذهِ الطِّفلةِ المُلتاعَة
(أنتَ تَعْرِفُ أنَّكَ قد لا تَراها ثانيةً
وأنَّكَ حينَ تعودُ إلى حَيْفا لَنْ تَجِدَها هُناك)

ماذا قالت لَكَ وهي تُودِّعُكَ
ماذا وَعَدْتَها وأنتَ تُوَدِّعُها
كَيْفَ أمْكَنَكَ أنْ تَبْتَسِم دونَ اكتراثٍ لأسْيِجَةِ الحُدودِ الشّائكة
وهي تَلْتَفُّ على قَلْبِكَ ـ ومياهُ البَحْرِ مالِحة...

كَيْفَ أمْكَنَك
كَيْفَ أمْكَنَك...
يا ابن الحَرام!

In Shatila

"There's no dignity here,"
the old woman tells you,
the one who left Haifa when she was nine months old.
She's sixty-five now
and standing in the swelter
outside her "house" in the camp.
She says it all
in just a couple of seconds.
She says it all
in just four words.

Rivers of regret,
years of agony that drown
in just four words.

You look at her bent back and think of the pines on Mount Carmel.
You look into her eyes and remember the kindness of the coast
while she complains to you about the faucets
and the brackish water that comes out of them.
And all you can do is smile as you open your heart
to this lovesick child.
You know you won't see her again:
She won't be there
when you head back to Haifa.

What did she tell you as she said her goodbyes?
What did you promise her as you said yours?
How could you smile, indifferent
to the brackish water of the sea
while the barbed wire wrapped around your heart?

How could you,
you son of a bitch?

مرثاة طفل نائم

I

يا بُنَيَّ، أنا قادِمٌ مِنْ ذاكِرةِ مَقْتولينَ
تَخْلِطُ بَيْنَ الطِّفْلِ النّائمِ والطِّفْلِ القَتيل
يا بُنَيَّ، لكنَّكَ ما زِلْتَ نائماً
الحَقْلُ مُسْتَيْقِظٌ مِنْ حَوْلِكَ في اللَّوْحَة
وأنا، بَعْدَ مُنْتَصَفِ اللَّيل، مَريضٌ ومُسْتَيْقِظٌ
في هذا الشَّمالِ البارد
أَسْمَعُ نَقْرَ المَطَرِ المُعْتِم
وأنتَ غافٍ لا تَسْمَعُ المَطَرَ ولا هَواجِسي
مِنْ أَيْنَ لي رِضاكَ لأنام؟
الحَقْلُ مُسْتَيْقِظٌ مِنْ حَوْلِك
ومِثلي يُفَكِّرُ في رَقْدَتِكَ الطَّويلةِ في الألوانِ الزِّيتيّةِ
بِيَدِ الرَّسام
وهي تُغَطّيكَ بِطَبَقَةٍ مِنَ الهَواءِ الدّاكِن
أنتَ نائمٌ الآنَ مِثْلَ طِفْلٍ قَتيل.

II

الهواءُ ثَقيلٌ في اللَّوْحَة
ولا يُسْعِفُني النَّظَرُ
ولَيْسَ لي بأسُ أَنْ أَراك

أَسْتَسْلِمُ للغَبَشِ
وأَنْهار.

Elegy for a Sleeping Child

I.

Son, I come from the memory
of the ones who've been killed—
it can't tell the difference
between a sleeping child
and a murdered child.
But you're still asleep, my son,
though the field's awake all around you in the painting.
And I'm still up, past midnight,
feeling sick in this cold northern land
and listening to the dark rain beating.
You're still asleep, and you can't hear the rain
or my misgivings.
Where can I find
such contented sleep?
The field's awake around you.
Like me, it's thinking
of your long sleep in the colors of the artist,
who covers you now
with a layer of dark air.

You're sleeping now
like a murdered child.

II.

The air's heavy in the painting,
and my eyes do not help me:
I don't have
the strength to see you.

Failing,
I surrender to the darkness.

تَعِبَ المُعَلَّقون

I

تَعِبَ المُعَلَّقون
أَنْزِلْنا
لِنَسْتَريح.

نَجُرُّ تَواريخَ
لا أَرْضَ ولا سَماء.

يا رَب
أَرِحْ ذَبيحَتَك.

II

لَمْ تَكُنْ لَكَ أُمٌّ ولَمْ يَكُنْ لَكَ أَبٌ
ولَمْ تَرَ إِخْوَتَك
مُعلَّقينَ بِمِخْلَبِ الفَجْرِ البارِدِ
لَمْ تُحِبَّ إنساناً
لَمْ يَهْجُركَ إنسانٌ
ولَمْ يَأْكُل مِنْ يَدِكَ المَوْت

أنتَ لَنْ تَفْهَمَ عَذابَنا.

III

لَسْتُ المَلِك داود
لأَجْلِسَ عِنْدَ بابِ النَّدَم
أُنَوِّحُ لكَ المَزاميرَ
بَعْدَ الخَطايا.

VI

أَنْزِلْني
أُريدُ أَنْ أَسْتَريح.

Exhausted on the Cross

The ones hanging
are tired,
so bring us down
and give us some rest.

We drag histories behind us
here
where there's neither land
nor sky.

Lord,
sharpen your knife
and give your sacrifice its rest.

* * *

You had no mother or father
and you never saw your brothers
hanging
from the cold talons of dawn.
You loved no one
and no one ever abandoned you
and death never ate from your hands.
You cannot know our pain.

* * *

I'm not King David—
I won't sit at the gate of regret
and sing you psalms of lamentation
after the sins.

* * *

Bring me down,
let me have my rest.

إنّه البحر

الأملُ المَرْصودُ لليأس
اليأسُ الناجي مِنَ الأمَل

تَلاشَتْ أوراقُ هذا البَحر
شَجَرتُهُ الوحيدةُ تَقرَعُها ريحٌ صَرْصَر
(تَهُبُّ مِنْ مَخْطوطةٍ تُراثِيّة)

إنّه البَحر
الأمَلُ المُوَشّى باليأس
اليأسُ المُقَطَّرُ مِنَ الأمَل.

The Sea

Hope devoted to despair,
despair delivered from hope.

The leaves of this sea scattered,
its only tree
buffeted by a gale
that blew from an ancient manuscript.

The sea:
hope embroidered with despair,
despair distilled from hope.

أحياناً أستيقظ

أَسْتَيْقِظُ أَحياناً مِنَ النّوم
فأجِدُ أَنَّ ألفَ سَنةٍ مَرَّتْ

كُلُّ ما كانَ لي صِلَةٌ بِهِ
يَبْدو سَحيقاً غَطَّتْهُ طَبَقاتٌ مِنَ النِّسيان.

لكِنَّ الواقعَ، هذا الدُّبَّ النّائمَ في الثَّلج
ما زال يُناديني بِاسْمي
الذي كانَ لي قَبْلَ ألفِ سَنة.
لو مَرَّةً أجرؤُ ولا أَرُدُّ عَليه
لو أقولُ لَهُ
ألفُ سَنةٍ مَرَّتْ وأنتَ لا تَدري.

Sometimes I Wake

Sometimes I wake from sleep
to find a thousand years have passed.

And everything I had a tie to
seems ancient, covered
by layers of oblivion.

But reality, this bear sleeping in the snow,
is still calling me by my name,
the one I had a thousand years ago.
What if, just once, I dared
to offer no reply?
Or what if, just once, I told him:
"A thousand years have passed
and you don't even know it."

قصيدة جندي متنكِّر

آخِرُ مَرَّةٍ كَتَبْتُ شِعراً
قَبْلَ ثَلاثَةِ آلافِ سَنَة
كُنْتُ أيامَها جُندياً مُتَنكِّراً بَعْدَ حَرْبٍ لَمْ يَصِلْهُ خَبَرُ انْتِهائها
وها أنا الآنَ أُحاوِلُ مِنْ جَديد؛
غُبارُ السَّنواتِ مِثْلَ غُبارِ المَقابِر
أخرجُ مِنَ الأرض كالبِذْرَةِ تَتَفَتَّقُ
كالبُرْعُمِ يَتَفَتَّحُ في الغُصْن
كالأموات
يَنْتَشِرونَ في أرضٍ لَيْسَ فيها سِوى الأموات.

A Poem by a Soldier in Disguise

The last time I wrote poetry
was three thousand years ago.
Back then, I was a soldier in disguise,
a soldier who didn't know the war was over,
and now here I am
trying to write all over again.
The dust of the years is like the dust of tombs.
I emerge from the earth like a seed bursting,
like a bud unfurling on the branch,
like the dead
who spread across a land
only death inhabits.

في الآستانة

جئتُ الآستانة مُتَنَكِّراً
لَمْ أشأ أنْ أحُلَّ ضَيْفاً على السُّلطان
لا أُريد أنْ أُفسِدَ كأسَ الشّاي هذا
بالعاجِ المُتآكِلِ في قُلوبِ الحاشِية.

البَشَرُ هُم أنفسُهُم
قَشِّر اللُّغات تَجِدْ رِجالاً ونِساءً
في كُلِّ مَكان.

لكِنْ مَنْ كنتُ سَأكونُ بِلا كلماتي؟
الصَّباحُ أجَّلَ الرِّحْلَةَ
والليلُ قالَ: أنا الرِّحْلَةُ والرّاحِلون.

ثُمَّ رأيتُ النّاسَ يَدْخُلونَ في العَدَم أفواجاً.

In Constantinople

I came to Constantinople in disguise.
I didn't want to be the Sultan's guest,
I didn't want to ruin this cup of tea
with ivory that corroded
in the hearts of his entourage.

People are simply people.
Peel off the languages, and all you'll find
is women and men.

But who would I have been without my words?
Morning delayed the journey,
and night said: "I'm the journey, and everyone in it."

Then I saw them
—the people—
entering the void in throngs.

رايتي المهزومة

لو قُدِّرَ لي أَنْ أَعود
فَلَنْ أَعودَ تَحْتَ رايةٍ أُخرى
أُعانِقُكِ بِيَدَيْنِ مَقْطوعَتَيْن
لا أُريدُ أَجْنِحَةً في الجَنَّة
أُريدُ مَراقِدَكُم عِنْدَ ضِفَّة النَّهر
أُريد الأَزَلَ على طاولةِ الفُطور
مع الخُبْزِ والزَّيْت
أُريدُكِ أَنتِ
يا أَرضُ
يا رايَتي المَهْزومَة.

My Defeated Banner

If I could come back,
I wouldn't come under any other banner.
I'd still embrace you
with two severed hands.
I don't want wings in paradise,
I just want your graves by the river.
I want eternity at the breakfast table
with the bread and oil.
I want *you*—
earth,
my defeated banner.

Gloria Gervitz

Migrations
Poem, 1976-2020

TRANSLATED BY MARK SCHAFER

NYRB/POETS

Migrations: Poem, 1976–2020
By Gloria Gervitz
Translated by Mark Schafer

Migrations is considered by critics to be a masterpiece of modern Mexican literature. Winner of the 2019 Pablo Neruda Ibero-American Poetry Prize, it is an epic journey in free verse through the individual and collective memories of Jewish women emigrants from Eastern Europe, a conversation that ranges across two thousand years of poetry, a bridge that spans the oracles of ancient Greece and the markets of modern Mexico, a prayer that blends the Jewish and Catholic liturgies, a Mexican woman's reclamation through poetry of her own voice and erotic power. In its reach, audacity, and astonishing vitality, Gervitz's extraordinary life's work bears comparison to the achievements of HD, Lorine Niedecker, Ezra Pound and Walt Whitman. Its voice is a collective as much as an individual voice: the voice of generations of women as well as one woman.

In an interview with Mark Schafer in 2021, reproduced in this book (translated by Mark and Ruby Fernández), Gloria Gervitz said:

> I began to write *Migraciones* at the beginning of September of 1976. I had a few words, a few lines that start the poem – 'en las migraciones de los claveles rojos donde revientan cantos de aves picudas / y se pudren las manzanas antes del desastre' – and then the next two or three lines. I especially had those first two lines in my mind, but they didn't really make much sense to me. I decided to write them down, and it was like opening a faucet. Of course, I never knew that I was entering what turned out to be a life's project. If you ask me exactly what those two lines mean, I still don't know. I honestly don't know – even now, after more than 44 years.
>
> Sometimes I feel that I'd like to be, say, ten years younger, with the poem the way it is now. But I know I couldn't have written the poem the way it is now if I weren't the age I am now. I needed all that life experience to be able to write *Migraciones*. I think time was a deciding factor in this last version of the poem. I also know that there are some people who prefer the other versions and perhaps will always prefer other versions; they feel more comfortable when the poem was divided into different parts. But I do know, deep down, that the way I left it in this last version is the way the poem wanted to be left. In a way, I needed a whole lifetime to do this.

When Mark submitted his translation of the final instantiation of *Migrations* for consideration, I was immediately struck by the originality and ambition of Gervitz's endeavor – what you might call its epic intimacy – and by the finesse of Schafer's translation. The fact that she conceived and wrote and reconceived and rewrote this one poem over so many years is evidence of her single-minded devotion to her work, as realised in this particular work.

Edwin Frank for New York Review Books

Migraciones (extracto)

y quizás
    y esto que soy

                y cambia
           y está en el centro

la intensidad de lo que es

           así entra ella en la Mikveh
           así se sumerge
           así la ofrenda
                 así

                 en el corazón del agua

From *Migrations*

and maybe
       and what I am

               and it changes
       and lies at the center

the intensity of what it is

       this is how she enters the Mikveh
       this is how she immerses herself
       this is how she makes the offering
                     this is how

                       in the heart of the water

y ahí

   ahí metida
     en ese cuerpo
de vieja
    yo

   más mortal
que nunca

   y el cuerpo

     áspera
    textura
     de simiente
      de hoja

    la piel

      con las manchas
    de la tierra

y los días allí
      uno
  y otro

   y otro

     ¿y si esto fuera sólo
un sueño?

and there

    placed there
        in that old woman's
body
  I

  more mortal
than ever

 and the body

     rough
   surface
    of sprouts
     of leaves

      her skin

       mottled
     with earth

and the days there
         one
  and another

     and another

      and if this were just
a dream?

di
  dime

tú que me conoces

tú que eres más yo
          que yo

tú que me entiendes

          porque yo a ti
      no te entiendo

    tú sí
tú

   dime
dime

      dime

tell
   tell me

you who know me

you who are more I
              than I am

you who understand me

              because you I
        don't understand you

    you   yes
you

    tell me
tell me

        tell me

      y el cuerpo

no deja
   no me deja

   no se deja entender

       y no se imagina
          no se imagina

lo que nos está pasando

    and the body

doesn't let
    doesn't let me

    doesn't let itself be understood

            and we can't imagine
                  can't imagine

what's happening to us

   y en lo sola
      y conmigo

     en lo solo terco
  y vanidoso

     esta yo

      a la que tanto quiero
         y tanto me quiere

    y me mira
     y se mira

y se fascina
    mirándose

     con sus aretes de cuarzo
    sus perlas

    sus broches de París

     me mira
       y no ve

       a la mujer gorda
          y vieja

      que soy

         ¿y yo si la veo?

and in her loneliness
    and with me

    in his loneliness stubborn
and vain

    this I

    I love so dearly
        and who loves me so dearly

and looks at me
    and looks at herself

looking at herself
    in fascination

    with her quartz earrings
    her pearls

    her brooches from Paris

    looks at me
        and doesn't see

    the fat old
        woman

    I am

        and I do I see her?

      y los otros

¿qué ven
      cuando me ven?

        and everyone else

what do they see

           when they see me?

    y en la calle
el sol
        y la vida

      a manos llenas

    como si sobrara
    como si fuera

        para siempre

          y el cuerpo aquí
                atrapado

                      y yo allí
          en ese cuerpo

          yo que no sé
      y no quiero
   saber

       que estoy
            vieja

    and in the street
sun
      and life

      in abundance

      as if there were plenty
      as if it were

          forever

          and the body trapped
                    here

                    and I'm there
           in that body

           I who don't know
      and don't want
    to know

        that I'm
           old

    ¿qué atajos

qué camino

  qué es esto
que siento?

    ¿a dónde
este naufragio

    estas palabras
      estos huesos

  a dónde?

        ¿qué hago aquí?

      what shortcuts

what path

    what's this
I'm feeling?

    where's this
shipwreck headed

   these words
     these bones?

   where?

      what am I doing here?

    el insomnio casi toca
la perfección

                estoy bien despierta en el sueño

    son las tres de la mañana
           y tengo miedo

    ¿esto es ser vieja
           ¿es así?

   my insomnia approaches
perfection

                I'm wide awake in my dream

  it's three in the morning
            and I'm afraid

  this is what it is to be old?
                  it's like this?

         y se me viene
de pronto
         una nostalgia

              acaso un tedio
                   de otra yo también

         olvidada

         y grito

            y la pequeña
         la apenas
vieja

      grita

            ¿yo?

                ¿ésta
            soy
                yo?

    and suddenly
a nostalgia
        comes over me

        perhaps the boredom
            of another me also

      forgotten

  and I cry out

      and she
    the almost
old woman

    cries out

          me?

           is
        she
           me?

    de ti las todas palabras
digo

  y el cuerpo
    viejo girasol
      se inclina
          ante la caricia

    se dobla
  tímido
    leve
se dobla

  ante ti

    las palabras
      son tuyas

    desde ti
  te acogen

desde ti
  su vuelo

      ¿no las oyes?

          ¿es que ya no me oyes?

    all the words are yours
I say

    and the body
        old sunflower
            bows
                under the caress

        bends
      shy
        gently
      bends

before you

        the words
            are yours

    from you
  they gather you in

from you
    their flight

           don't you hear them?

                  don't you hear me anymore?

Unexpected Vanilla
   By Lee Hyemi
      Translated by Soje

Unexpected Vanilla is a sensual, surrealist collection by Lee Hyemi, a feminist poet based in South Korea. Equally sensuous and sensitive is Soje's queer translation from Korean to English. Filled with bittersweet moments, the tactile, charged and dreamlike poems in this collection detail the subtleties of exchange: that of intimacies, of worlds, of fluids.

In her preface to the collection, Lee Hyemi writes:

> There is always an exchange of fluids
> at the critical moment when a relationship deepens.
> Holding the fish jar in which alphabet letters swim
> I step into the world of the second person.

This exchange of liquids often involves sex, but intercourse can be non-sexual as well: drinking tea or alcohol, going to the beach, sitting in the same tub, crying, feeling your lover's sweat on your palm. In this way, Lee explores a wide variety of relationships, attractions and sensations. Her erotically charged, surrealist sensibility can be traced back to the paintings of Leonor Fini, a bisexual Argentinian artist whom she admires. Indeed, her poems and the lovers within often have the stillness of a painting and the same observational distance. The poems speak to a kind of listlessness that can occur when you are moved by somebody without necessarily knowing what that moving is.

Lee Hyemi, born in 1988, is the author of three poetry collections and an essay collection. At eighteen, she was one of the youngest winners of the JoongAng Literary Newcomer's Prize. Soje's English translation of *Unexpected Vanilla*, Lee's second collection, was shortlisted for the 2021 National Translation Award in Poetry. Soje was instrumental in bringing Lee Hyemi to the attention of Tilted Axis Press, having already translated several of her poems for outlets including *Words Without Borders*, *Asymptote* and *Korean Literature Now*.

In her 'world of the second person', which feels clandestine but safe from the threat of exposure, Lee explores the Korean language's scope for ambiguous gendering. The task of the queer translator is to feel out the subtleties with respect, as one does in life, and not presume heterosexuality. Soje came to the collection as part of an exercise during a translation workshop. They were asked to translate

a poet they had never read before and a title caught their eye: *Unexpected Vanilla*. Immersing themselves in Lee's poetics, Soje was instinctively drawn to it and knew they found their next project.

Lee subverts the titular 'vanilla' norm without denying its pleasures. She points out that what we now take for granted may well change in the future, and what is now considered normal might soon become outmoded. Kink or vanilla: Lee's poems dissolve the perceived difference between both. There is no either/or, it simply is. And like vanilla ice cream, the poems in this collection are sweet, melt on the tongue and cling to the lips long after the collection has been put aside.

Soje, Theodora Danek, Kristen Vida Alfaro and Tice Cin for Tilted Axis Press

숨의 세계

잠든 이의 코에 손을 대어본 사람은
영혼을 믿는 자다 깊은 밤,
숨은 수풀을 지나 진창에 흐르고 깊이
젖어 고단한 채 돌아온다

녹기 시작한 발자국을 따라가듯
먼저 잠든 이의 숨에 입김을 잇대어
호흡의 빛살을 엮으면

안쪽은 불타는 숲 바깥은
휘도는 눈보라

사이를
숨은 새처럼 날아간다
문득, 다른 궤도로 진입하는 행성처럼

안겨 잠든 새벽에만 들리는 소리가 있어
하나의 검불이 흰 들판으로
순하게 내려앉는 소리
젖은 귀를 어루만지는
외바퀴 소리

가볍고 약하고 투명하게
매 순간 새로 태어나는 심연을 바라보며

그 속에서 얼굴을 지운다
뒤섞여 드리우는
점차 짙어지며 스며드는
공기의 매듭들

World of Breaths

Whoever has ever put their hand under the nose
of a sleeping person believes in souls Deep at night
breaths drift past a forest and flow in the mud,
returning soaked and weary

If you weave the rays of respiration,
joining your breaths with the sleeper's
as if retracing footprints that have started to melt,

inside is the blazing forest
outside is the whirling blizzard

Like birds, breaths fly
in between the two
like planets suddenly entering another orbit

Some things you only hear at dawn, asleep embraced:
the sound of a dry leaf gently
falling on a white field,
the sound of a single wheel
stroking a wet ear

Watching the abyss constantly be reborn
lightly, weakly, clearly

you erase your face
The knots of air,
jumbled and suspended,
deepen and seep into each other

딸기잼이 있던 찬장

발끝을 힘껏 들고 높은 곳을 더듬어 충분히 붉은 것들을 맛보았어. 입가를 온통 물들인 채 한 쌍의 유두가 된 기분으로.

언니, 우린 분명 교묘히 어긋난 한 사람일 거야. 딸기의 어수선한 초록 왕관을 쓰고 이불 속에서 첫 몽정을 말하던 아침. 땀구멍마다 질긴 씨를 하나씩 슬어놓으며 우리는 함부로 은밀해지고 조금씩 말랑해졌지. 반투명 젤리 속 일렁이는 둘만의 왕국에서.

나에게 여분의 계절이 있다면, 부리가 사라지려는 새처럼 서둘러 속된 말들을 속삭이고 썩기 직전의 가장 달콤한 노래를 언니에게 선물했을 텐데. 분홍 만으로 이루어진 무지개를 뭉개고 죄의식의 묘한 기쁨으로 아침의 올빼미를 불러올 텐데.

손가락 사이로 달고 끈적한 것들이 흘러내릴 때, 감춰야할 것이 늘어버린 마음으로. 한 개의 입술이 더 있었다면, 한 쌍의 얇은 점막이 더 있었다면, 뒤 섞이며 짙어지는 맛들에 대해 함께 이야기할 수 있었을 텐데.

오늘은 그저 길게 두 팔을 벌리고 옛 붉음을 겪었지. 우리가 아직 숨겨진 단것을 사랑하던 그때.

The Cupboard with Strawberry Jam

We stood on our tiptoes and fumbled around the top shelf for a taste of those red red things. With mouths dyed all over, feeling like a pair of nipples.

Unni, we must be one person, cunningly divergent. The morning we wore the disheveled green crowns of strawberries and spoke of our first wet dreams under the covers. We laid a chewy seed in every pore, growing recklessly private and gradually tender. In the kingdom for two who sway inside translucent jelly.

If I had a spare season, I would've rushed to whisper vulgar words like a bird with a disappearing beak and gifted you the sweetest song on the verge of rot. I would've squished the all-pink rainbow and called the morning owl over with the strange joy of guilt.

Feeling like there was more to hide now as the sweet stickiness dripped between my fingers. If we had another pair of lips, another pair of thin mucous membranes, we could've talked about the flavors that deepen as they're mixed.

But today, simply with our arms spread wide, we experienced our ruddiness of old. Of the days when we loved what was hidden and sweet.

밀가루의 맛

얼음을 핥으며 오래 말을 아꼈지
케이크를 자르고 낮술을 마시던
창가에서

그 희고 연약한 윤곽을
망쳐놓으며 너는 없는 아름다움을
말했다 무심히 손을 휘저으며
미음과 리을 받침에 대해 이야기했지

나는 알곡처럼 선연하다 분명하여 부서지는
것들에 대해
같은 크기의 입자가 되어가는 것들에 대해

왜 부서져 떠돌다 싫은 덩어리로 마무리되는
것일까

입으로 불어도 손으로 쓸어도 자국을 남기던
눈송이들
얼어붙은 잔설이 회색으로 얼룩진 그
창가에서

흰 가루라면 무엇이든 슬프던 계절이 지나간다
눈처럼 녹아 사라질 줄 알았는데
끈질기게 혀에 붙어 끈적이는
더럽고 슬프고 무거운

Taste of Flour

We spared our words for a long time, licking ice
by the window where we cut cake and day drank

Ruining that fragile white outline
you spoke of nonexistent beauty
Carelessly waving your hands
you talked about the letters *f* and *l*

And I, about what crumbles from being clear and distinct like grains,
about what becomes uniform particles

Why do they crumble and wander and end up an awful lump

Those snowflakes stained whether I
blew on them or swept them away with my hand
We mourned every white powder
by the window where the refrozen snow was mottled gray

The season of such mourning passes by

I thought all powders would melt away like snow
but it stubbornly stuck to my tongue
So dirty and sad and heavy

뜻밖의 바닐라

귓바퀴를 타고 부드럽게 미끄러졌지. 미묘한 요철을 따라 흐르는, 그런 혀끝의 바닐라.

수없이 많은 씨앗들을 그러모으며 가장 보편적인 표정을 지니려. 두근거리며 이국의 이름을 외웠지. 그건 달콤에 대한 첫번째 감각. 사라지는 것들에 대한 각별한 취향.

녹아내리는 손과 무릎이 있었지. 차갑고 뜨겁게 흐르는, 접촉이 서로를 빚어낼때. 소리의 영토 안에서 나는 세로로 누운 꽃. 손끝에서 점차 태어나. 닿아 녹으며 섞이는, 품이라는 말.

그런 바닐라. 적당한 점도의 안구를 지니려. 모르는 사람을 나는 가장 사랑하지. 잃어버리는 순간 온 전해지는 눈꺼풀이 있었다. 순한 촉수를 흔들며 미끄러지다 홈뻑 쓰러지는.

Unexpected Vanilla

It glided along the groove of my ear. Vanilla on the tip of my tongue, dribbling down the subtle bumps.

We had to keep a neutral expression while scraping all those seeds. With a fluttering heart, we memorized the names of foreign countries. Our first sensation of sweetness. A special appetite for impermanent things.

Yes, some hands and knees were melting. We created each other, strokes running hot and cold. In the territory of sound I'm a flower reclining vertically. Blossoming before a fingertip. The word *embrace* melts and melds upon contact.

That type of vanilla. To keep my eyeballs moist, I love most whom I don't know. Some eyelids grew whole the moment we lost them. Slid and waved their gentle tentacles before falling, heavy with wet.

자취

잿가루가 춤추는 야적의 시절
발자국은 지붕을 가지지 못하여
긴 유랑은 언제나 절벽을 향한다

매자나무의 녹병 무늬를 더듬으며 간다
갈라진 이마에 붉은 속이 비치고
나는 한 움큼씩 가벼워지는구나
먼지로 가득 차 야윈 자루처럼

덤불을 헤치며 불기 남은 땅에 닿는다
분별없이 온기를 부려두고 떠났네 예전에
만난 적 있는 낯선 사람들

세밀하고 감촉할 수 없는 낌새가 되어
수많던 우리는 어디에 몸을 감췄나

나는 지워지며 점점 증식한다
속눈썹이 모두 사라질까 두렵다

어느새 나는 두 손을 한없이 숨기고 있구나
약제사가 종이에 분약을 싸듯이
으스러지고 불려가지 않으려

Trace

The time of field heaping when ashes dance
Footprints cannot have roofs
so long wanderings always head to a cliff

I touch the rust pattern on the barberry tree as I walk
Through the crack in my forehead my red insides
can be seen and I grow lighter by the handful
like a lean sack filled with dust

Pushing through thickets I reach the land
where strangers met before
left behind warmth indiscreetly

Where did we all hide our bodies,
having become detailed insensible inklings

I multiply as I am erased
I fear all my eyelashes will disappear

I didn't notice that I started hiding my hands
like the pharmacist wrapping powder medicine in paper
so I won't shatter and be swept away

넝쿨 꿈을 꾸던 여름

떨어진 능소화를 주워 눈에 비비니
원하던 빛 속이다

여름 꿈을 꾸고 물속을 더듬으면
너르게 펼쳐지는 빛의 내부

잠은 꿈의 넝쿨로 뒤덮여 형체를 잊은
오래된 성곽 같지

여름을 뒤집어 꿰맨 꽃
주홍을 내어주고 안팎을 바꾸면
땅속에 허리를 담근 채 다른 자세를 꿈꾸는
물의 잠시(暫時)

꽃은 물이 색을 빌려 꾸는 꿈
옛 꽃들에 둘러싸인 검은 돌벽 위로
생소한 돋기를 내뿜으며
무수히 가지를 뻗는 여름의 넝쿨

눈 없는 잎사귀들처럼
뜨거운 잠의 벽을 기어오르면

눈동자 위로 쏟아져 내리는
빛의 손가락들

입술을 뒤집고 숨을 참으니
원하던 꿈속, 물꿈 속

Summer, When I Dreamt of Vines

I pick up a fallen trumpet flower and rub it on my eyes
and now I'm inside the light as I wished

When I dream of summer and feel around the water
light's interior opens wide

Sleep is like an old castle
covered in vines, its silhouette forgotten

A flower created from flipping and stitching up summer
When the flower offers scarlet and turns itself inside out
the water's moment
dips its waist underground and dreams of a different position

A flower, a dream dreamt by water borrowing color
Spouting strange bumps
above the black stone wall surrounded by old blossoms,
the vines of summer extend countless tendrils

When I climb the wall of sultry sleep
like eyeless leaves

the fingers of light
pour onto my eyes

I roll my lips inward and hold my breath
and now I'm inside the dream, the water-dream as I wished

라라라, 버찌

버찌를 따러 갈 거예요 붉푸르게 얼룩진 것들만을 골라 주머니 가득 담을래요 버찌, 서로를 베껴 쓰는 빨강 빨강들 환한 밤 내내 버찌를 가득 물고 곤란한 키스를 나눌까요

꽃도 잎도 벗어던진 버찌는 오늘, 그저 한 알의 유희

아직 그의 버찌는 익어 터지지도 못했는데 진물 흐르도록 섞이지도 못했는데 뭉쳐진 초록만 베어 물고 계절이 다 지나가요 우리, 너무 일찍 수확되었죠 그의 입속에 내가 가진 물감을 한가득 풀어놓고 싶은, 얼룩지는, 버찌의 시간인데요

Lalala, Cherries

Hello, I'm going cherry picking I want to fill my pockets with only the ones stained dark Cherries are red copying another red Shall we fill our mouths with cherries and kiss naughtily knottily all night long

Cherries strip off their flowers and leaves Today they're just kernels of play

Her cherry hasn't even had a chance to ripen and burst, to schmooze and ooze We only got to bite into a clump of green And now the season's almost over We were harvested too soon I want to swirl my paints inside her mouth This is the time of cherries A time that stains

펨돔

방의 구석마다 물고기들이 자라나 날카로운 빛을 일구었어. 바늘자국으로 가득한 몸들. 도망쳤다 되돌아온 것들이 다시 머리채를 내밀어 상처를 갈구하네. 저 노동하는 성기들. 나의 그물 속에서 혼절하는 몸들. 파문을 향해 헤엄치는 젖은 비늘들을 봐. 걸어 잠근 문을 두드리는 부러진 손가락들을 봐. 다른 이의 주인이 되기 위해 떨리는 눈동자를 다정히 짓이길 때, 내 빛나는 물고기들이 묶인 발로 절규하지. 그건 두려움을 선물하는 일. 핏줄을 열어 솟구침을 확인하고서야 맹세를 다짐하는 내 아름다운 천민들이여. 방바닥 가득 퍼덕이는 이 비문들을 봐. 나는 반쯤 죽은 어제들을 종일 찢고 부수네. 두려움을 이끄는 더 큰 두려움으로.

Femdom

Fish grew in every corner of the room and cultivated a sharp light. Bodies riddled with needle marks. Those that fled and returned are sticking their heads out again and thirsting for scars. Those laboring genitals. Bodies fainting inside my net. Look at the wet scales swimming towards the ripples of expulsion. Look at the broken fingers knocking on the door bolted shut. When I tenderly trample on the trembling gaze of another being to become their master, all my luminous fish cry out with tied feet. That's the gift of fear. My beautiful low-lives, who pledge allegiance only after opening their veins and checking for a surge. Look at these epitaphs flopping all over the bedroom floor. All day long I rip and break the half-dead yesterdays. With fear led by an even larger fear.

The River in the Belly
  By Fiston Mwanza Mujila
    Translated by J. Bret Maney

Deep Vellum Publishing and Phoneme Media came into existence at roughly the same time, in 2013, some 1,500 miles apart across North America, in Dallas and Los Angeles respectively. At that time, Deep Vellum was primarily focused on fiction, and Fiston Mwanza Mujila's prize-winning novel *Tram 83*, translated by Roland Glasser, epitomized our shared commitment to publishing voices outside the literary mainstream. When Phoneme became an imprint of Deep Vellum Publishing in late 2019, one of my first hopes was that I might have the chance to be involved in bringing Fiston's poetry into English. Deep Vellum founder Will Evans was a step ahead of me, having already acquired the manuscript that would become *The River in the Belly* in English.

I first met Fiston on his US book tour in support of *Tram 83*, in the fall of 2015. It was a typical Los Angeles fall, the golden light of a warm afternoon ceding to the chill of dusk, and I gave Fiston a ride across the city back to his hotel, each of us enunciating slowly – him in French and me in English – so that the other could understand. The reading in Los Angeles was Fiston's penultimate event in the US, and though he was clearly tired after several weeks on the road our conversation was almost as wide-ranging, serious and hilarious as *The River in the Belly*, spanning literature, jazz, American and Congolese cuisine, and the benevolent anonymity and generative randomness of our respective neverending cities. We cruised through Little Bangladesh and Koreatown to Hollywood, and I occasionally pointed out landmarks of dubious note. We had several friends in common from across sub-Saharan Africa, and we shared the latest news we'd heard, diasporic tidings. I had just published Christopher Schaefer's translation of Roland Rugero's *Baho!*, the first Burundian novel to appear in English, and I had recently acquired Richard Ali A Mutu's novella *Mr. Fix-It*, which I was struggling to find a translator to render into English from Lingala. I was eager to read Fiston's poetry, and told him so. I cut up South Fairfax Avenue through Little Ethiopia and then over the surface streets of Tehrangeles, and despite the brevity of our encounter it seemed like we had traversed half the world in the hour it took to traverse the city. I felt a pang of sadness – perhaps the same sodade Fiston evokes in 'Solitude 99 or Esperanza Club' – when he hopped out of my car at his hotel in Santa Monica with a nimble au revoir.

The River in the Belly was originally contracted by Deep Vellum as one section of a selected poems. When I read the draft of that manuscript which J. Bret Maney delivered, I recognised three clear volumes, and I knew that two of them – this one and a book of kasala poems, forthcoming from Deep Vellum's Phoneme Media imprint in 2024 – could stand most powerfully on their own. Writing about *The River in the Belly*, Forrest Gander celebrates its defiance of categorization, embedding a question in the very term he coins to describe it, a 'raucous, electrifying what-is-it?'. Is it a 'memoir, broken novel, poem series? Or is it mainly a protest against the way that dreams can vanish like migrating birds?' The answer, I think – and I suspect Forrest would agree – is that Fiston's 'solitudes' belong to a category – perhaps even a genre – entirely their own. *The River in the Belly* introduces the solitude as a freer, iterative African canto, inspired by the improvisatory nature of jazz and the chaos, at turns jubilant and tragic, of the poet's Lubumbashi. There is an element of Congolese confessionalism here, alongside myth-making and joke-telling, history and lyric. The solitude is a deeply personal form, and at the same time its conversational character suggests a communal dialogue. Fiston's performances, sometimes in collaboration with jazz musicians, foreground the improvisatory nature of the genre as well as its give-and-take with the reader or listener: the solitude is a form that feeds on the energy of its subject matter as well as that of its audience.

Collaborating with translator J. Bret Maney has been one of the great pleasures of my work as an editor. He is a natural scholar whose intellect serves the poetry at hand, rather than weighing it down. It was thrilling to chase down the more obscure historical details Fiston liberally sprinkles throughout his book, and to query our community for its assistance translating the bits and bobs of German, Lingala, Katanga Swahili, and even Kriolu that appear throughout the book. I will forever recall reading later drafts of *The River in the Belly* aloud, to my partner and infant, in the sand dunes at Dillon Beach, in Northern California, a year into the pandemic, with the lapping of the waves serving as a sort of metronome, interrupted by months-old gurgles I interpreted as appreciation. It was then, reading the book through in its entirety, that the importance of its publication came fully into focus: not only is *The River in the Belly* important because it represents one of the mere handful of books of sub-Saharan African poetry to ever appear in translation into English, these poems – and the new form they introduce – are revolutionary and essential. We English-language readers need them. Like the river they describe and embody, they are restless and ever changing, bearing infinite re-readings. Like the river Fiston describes early in the book, as well as the poet himself, *The River in the Belly* is 'a confounded malingerer, dirty and immense, mournful and malign'.

Shook for Phoneme Media, Deep Vellum

Le Fleuve dans le Ventre [Extraits]

SOLITUDE 33

la poésie (disons) le rêve est tout ce qui nous reste en ce temps de crise…

Selected Solitudes from *The River in the Belly*

SOLITUDE 33

poetry (let's say) the dream is all we still have in this time of crisis…

SOLITUDE 35

c'est en homme démangé que je retourne vers mon passé
toujours en homme frustré que je marche vers mon destin
seul, gémissant en ré mineur et maladroit
tel que je suis sorti du ventre de ma mère
des brisures de ma part en part
de mon charbon de corps maigrichon et chat échaudé
peut-être par mégarde qu'il aurait fallu que je naisse Lazare
pour renaître de mes écorces
trois jours après ma pourriture
peut-être…

SOLITUDE 35

as a man with an itch, I return to my past
as a still-frustrated man, I lurch into my future
alone, bawling in D minor, and as klutzy
as the day I came out of my mother's womb
my scrawny, charcoal body crosshatched
by cracks, once bitten, twice shy
perhaps, by mistake, I wasn't born Lazarus
to be reborn from my rind
three days into my putrefaction
perhaps…

SOLITUDE 49

On doit être identique aux autres, sinon on manque sa croûte, sinon on va aboyer avec les chiens, sinon on décroche et on largue sa chair par la fenêtre de la salle à manger. Le nouveau monde exige que nous soyons les fils d'un même père et d'une même mère, que nous soyons des sœurs et des frères siamois, des jumeaux au centimètre près… Et le fusil n'est pas (et n'a jamais été) entre nos mains. Nous sommes dressés contre mur, jambes écartées, les bras en l'air. Le drame c'est qu'on n'est pas au cinéma.

SOLITUDE 49

We must be no different from the others, or we go unfed, or we're sent to howl with the dogs, or we unpin and drop our own skins out the lunchroom window. The new world demands we be the children of the same father and mother, conjoined siblings, twins to the nearest sixteenth of an inch… and that the rifle not be (no have ever been) in our hands. We are stood up against the wall, legs apart, hands up. The tragedy is that this is not the movies.

SOLITUDE 65

J'étais un grand naïf. Je croyais que le fleuve Zaïre m'appartenait, que le fleuve Zaïre était un bien privé, une propriété familiale au même titre que la machine à coudre à pédale de marque Singer dont ma mère avait hérité de sa tante ou les disques 33 tours que mon père collectionnait…

Je croyais que je pouvais couper le fleuve en quatre, le foutre dans mes bagages, le fourrer dans mes chaussettes et prendre le premier train, direction Rio de Janeiro. Je croyais que je pouvais le déplacer, en distribuer des miettes à des copains ou le séjourner dans le désert du Sahara.

Chaque soir, à peine rentré de son travail, mon père m'assiégeait: Mwanza, viens ici ! Que feras-tu de ton fleuve lorsque tu deviendras adulte ? Est-ce que tu as déjà donné à manger à ton fleuve ? Il a encore quel âge ce fleuve-là ? Dis-moi, il est de quelle nationalité ton fleuve ? Tu attendras dix-huit ans pour aller vivre avec ton fleuve. Ne fais pas entrer le fleuve dans ta chambre. Tu sais bien que tu ne sais pas encore nager et Noé ne viendra pas te délivrer en cas de noyade.

Dimanche était une journée de bénédiction. Nous nous asseyions dans la véranda en quatrième de couverture son gramophone crachotant le soul makossa. Il sifflait ses bouteilles de bière, fumait ses cigarettes Gauloises et me racontait avec son accent d'enseignant de français langue étrangère comment le fleuve Zaïre danse la samba avant de se défenestrer dans l'océan. Il me surnommait « l'enfant de la Léna » prétextant que j'étais un fleuve le jour de ma naissance, que j'étais né non loin du fleuve russe de la Léna et que maman, dans l'autre vie, était la Léna. « La femme-fleuve », renchérissait-il le regard cloué au plafond comme les Saints sur les cartes postales qu'il ramenait d'Italie.

À l'époque, j'étais beau, riche, insensible, orgueilleux et pervers comme nos dictateurs africains. Tous les gamins du quartier étaient sous mes bottes. Ils venaient dès six heures du matin me rendre visite avec leurs petits-déjeuners

SOLITUDE 65

I was hopelessly naive. I thought the Zaire River was mine, the Zaire River was my personal property, that it was my family's just like the Singer sewing machine my mother had inherited from her aunt of the LPs my father collected were…

I thought I could slice the river in quarters, ram it in my suitcase, stuff it inside my socks, and catch the next train for Rio de Janeiro. I thought it was a moveable feast, that I could dole it out as crumbs to my pals, or send it on a getaway to the Sahara.

My father used to accost me every evening when he got home from work: "Mwanza, come here! What are you going to do with your river after you grow up? Have you fed your river tonight? How old is that river of yours, again? Tell me, what country does your river belong to? You can't live with your river until you turn eighteen. Your river is not allowed in your bedroom. You know perfectly well you don't know how to swim and Noah won't save you if you start to drown."

Sundays were a godsend. We sat on the veranda, makossa crackling from my father's record player. He sucked down his bottles of beer, smoked his Gauloises, and told me—with the impeccable accent of a teacher of French as a foreign language—how the Zaire River dances the samba before offing itself in the ocean. He nicknamed me "Lena's Boy", claiming I was a river on the day I was born, that I was born not far from the Lena River in Russia, and that mother, in a former life, was the Lena. "The river-woman," he added, his gaze turned upwards like the saints on the postcards he used to bring back from Italy.

In those days, I was dashing, rich, implacable, full of pride, and wicked like our African dictators. I made all the neighborhood kids squirm beneath my thumb. They would appear on my doorstep as early as 6am to pay me their respects with their breakfasts and pocket money. I made them get down on

et leur argent de poche. Ils s'agenouillaient, me suppliaient et en contrepartie, je leur narrais toutes les anecdotes sur le fleuve Zaïre, mes origines russes et la psychologie de certains fleuves dont le Yang-Tsé-Kiang. Cela dit, j'étais le plus misérable pendant le cours de géographie. Le professeur, un vieil ami de mon père, sachant depuis toujours ma passion pour le fleuve et incapable de traduire en justice son pote pour une histoire de disque, décidait de me faire payer les pots cassés de leur amitié.

Au lieu de parler de Groenland et des villes portuaires comme le voulait le programme de géo, il dépensait sa salive à dénigrer le fleuve. Il débarquait dans la salle de classe, se ruait vers moi, me fixait des yeux avant de lancer, par exemple : « le fleuve Zaïre est une petite rivière de rien du tout – le fleuve Zaïre a mal au ventre – le fleuve Zaïre est un déchet – un fleuve qui ne sert à rien – un fleuve paresseux – un fleuve-bidon – un fleuve troué... »

Ses paroles résonnaient comme des coups de canon. Mes larmes rivalisaient alors avec les chutes du Niagara. Les autres élèves n'ignorant pas les sévices auxquels j'étais livré en pâture ricanaient, susurraient et reprenaient en chœur les phrases de mon bourreau. Ce qui mettait un peu de sel dans la verve de l'orateur, poursuivant sa fatwa contre le fleuve, mon fleuve Zaïre : « un petit fleuve abominable – un fleuve sale et lugubrement grotesque – un fleuve par accident – que foutent les Américains au lieu de nous lessiver ce fleuve ? »

L'humiliation était totale. J'avais envie de crever, de me jeter du haut de la tour de la Télévision Nationale... Le fleuve Zaïre représentait beaucoup pour moi. C'était mon fleuve, un fleuve à moi tout seul. J'en avais la foi, la ferme assurance, la certitude cartésienne...

Une après-midi, le géographe s'activa pendant quarante minutes à faire des comparaisons fortuites entre les différents fleuves du monde et donc, à rechigner sur le fleuve qui était le mien, « un fleuve minable, un fleuve sans avenir, un fleuve-rivière, syphilitique, frappé de malaria, malencontreux et scabreux par-dessus le marché noir de l'histoire. » Et c'en était trop. Le même soir, je fis rapport à mes parents qui prirent l'affaire au sérieux. Le lendemain déjà, papa m'accompagna à l'école. Le proviseur convoqua le professeur en question. À la suite des empoignades, on décida d'une confrontation avec l'ensemble de la classe. Monsieur le proviseur demanda à la classe, s'il était vrai que le professeur dépensait toute son énergie à cracher des insanités

their knees and beg, and, in return, I told them stories about the Zaire River, my Russian roots, and the psychological profiles of various rivers, including the Yangtze. In spite of that, in geography class I was the most miserable of students. The teacher, an old friend of my father's, had long known of my passion for the river. Unwilling to confront my father over a dispute about some records, he decided to make me pay the price for their broken friendship.

Instead of talking about Greenland and port cities, as the geography curriculum dictated, he wasted his breath bashing my river. He would plunge into our classroom, sail straight to my desk, and look me right in the eye while saying things like "the Zaire River is a piddling stream – the Zaire River has a bellyache – the Zaire River is a dud – a river that's good for nothing – a lazy river – a phony river – a river full of holes…"

His words hit me like cannonballs. My tears rivaled the falls at Niagara. The other pupils, perfectly aware of the torture to which I was being subjected, snickered, whispered to one another, and took up the chorus of my executioner's insults. Which only added fuel to the fire of his oratory. He continued his fatwa against the river, my Zaire River: "an abominable pipsqueak of a river – a morosely grotesque, polluted river – an accidental river – what in hell could the Americans be up to that they still haven't paved over this river?"

It was utter humiliation. I wanted to die, to throw myself off the top of the National Television tower… The Zaire River meant a lot to me. It was my river, a river I had all to myself. I had faith in my river, the firmest of assurances, Cartesian certainty…

One afternoon the geography teacher went on for forty minutes making arbitrary comparisons among the world's rivers, and, of course, slandering the one river that was mine, which he called "a paltry river, a river with no future, a rivulet sick with syphilis and malaria, and on top of that, one of the most singularly unlucky and filthy-minded rivers in history." It was too much. That very evening, I made a full report to my parents, who took the matter seriously. The next day father accompanied me to school. The principal summoned the teacher in question. After some hard words between them, it was decided to put the matter to the entire class. The principal asked my classmates if it was true that the teacher devoted all his energy to spewing

sur le fleuve. Les élèves qui savaient ce qu'ils risqueraient après son départ, conscients du caractère rancunier du géographe, nièrent les faits, ajoutant que c'est une fabulation de ma part, une fiction à part entière et je n'étais pas à mon premier forfait. Comme pour soigner leur image auprès du bourreau, sans se faire prier, des huées.

Deux jours plus tard, le gangster, de sa voix cassée par les cigarettes de seconde lèvre et autres breuvages en provenance de Brazza via le Beach Ngobila, myopie avancée, démarche Charlie Chaplin et tout de vert vêtu, reprit son réquisitoire.

– Si j'étais Président de la République, je donnerais bien ce fleuve aux Boliviens, le fleuve Congo discrédite notre pays, un fleuve sans valeur, un fleuve prêt à se suicider, un fleuve villageois, un fleuve à vendre, un fleuve qui ne sait même pas s'essuyer les babines et grammaticalement faux !

– Tu mens, criai-je a deux reprises, désespérément.
Des larmes…
Je sortis mon mouchoir…
Il continua, de plus belle…

– Le fleuve Zaïre est une mascarade, et d'ailleurs, à dire vrai, ce fleuve n'existe pas, le fleuve Zaïre n'a jamais existé, le fleuve Zaïre est une utopie. Où sont les Américains pour dégager cette saleté de ce beau pays ? J'irai personnellement voir Mobutu et je lui dirai « Excellence Monsieur le Président, sauf votre respect, partagez cette chose, donnez une partie aux Zambiens, une partie aux Thaïlandais, une partie à nos amis français, une partie à nos oncles de Belgique, une partie aux Angolais, aux Polonais, aux Tanzaniens… »

Je sentis comme des vomissements, des vertiges… Les élèves, des huées… Je me levai mécaniquement, pris mon cartable et sortis. Ce fut mon premier acte de désobéissance publique. Mes voisins de banc cessèrent de rire. Le géographe voulut me retenir par la main.

– Où vas-tu p'tit salaud !
– Rejoindre le fleuve !

rubbish about the river. My classmates, who well knew what they risked once the principal left, being aware of the geography teacher's spiteful disposition, denied everything, adding that it was a total fabrication of mine, a complete fiction, and not the first time I'd cried wolf. As if to burnish their image with my torturer, without even being asked to, they booed me.

Two days later, the gangster, whose voice was hoarse from black-market cigarettes and liquor from Brazza smuggled in via Ngobila Beach, behind his thick glasses, with the duck-like gait of Charlie Chaplin, and dressed entirely in green, resumed his inquisition:

"If I were president of the republic, I'd donate this river to the Bolivians without a second thought. The Zaire River is a discredit to our country, a worthless river, a river teetering on the brink of suicide, a dinky river, a river for sale, a river that doesn't even know how to lick its chops, and grammatically incorrect besides!"

"You lie!" I shouted, in desperation. "You lie!"
Tears…
I took out my handkerchief…
He went on, it got worse…

"The Zaire River is a masquerade, and besides—if we're going to be honest about it—the river doesn't even exist. The Zaire River has never existed. The Zaire River is a utopia, a no place. Where the heck are the Americans to flush this dirty thing out of our beautiful country? I will personally go see Mobutu, and tell him, 'Your Excellency, Mr. President, with all due respect, divvy this thing up, give some to the Zambians, some to the Thais, some to our friends in France, some to our uncles in Belgium, some to the Angolans, to the Poles, to the Tanzanians' …"

I felt like I was going to throw up, I was dizzy… The pupils booed and booed… I stood up mechanically, picked up my schoolbag, and left. That was my first act of public disobedience. My classmates stopped laughing. The geography teacher tried to stop me by the hand.

"Where are you going, you little bastard?"
"To rejoin the river!"

SOLITUDE 44

Qu'ils psalmodient le Brahmapoutre, qu'ils exhibent le Yang-Tsé-Kiang, qu'ils encensent le Zambèze, qu'ils affichent l'Euphrate, qu'ils pérorent la Meuse, qu'ils chantent le Guadalquivir, qu'ils élisent le Mississippi et ses gendres, à savoir l'Arkansas, le Missouri et l'Ohio, je brandirai le Congo, le seul fleuve qui déconcentre, le seul fleuve qui simule la tuberculose, le seul fleuve qui danse le tango, la salsa, le boléro, le flamenco et le cha-cha-cha, le seul fleuve qui vous rechigne, le seul fleuve qui broute de la viande, le seul fleuve qui se suicide dans l'océan, jambes jointes, bras croisés... Je donne ma main à couper, mon cou à trancher et mon corps à castrer s'il s'avère que je fais usage de faux. Déjà, je suis castré et minable tel le Limpopo à ses heures perdues. En tout état de cause, que craindrai-je ? La masturbation forcée, l'épreuve du kiambi ou l'assassinat déguisé en noyade dans les eaux de ce même fleuve ?

SOLITUDE 44

Let 'em praise the Brahmaputra, let 'em write home about the Yangtze, let 'em acclaim the Zambezi, they can flaunt the Euphrates, go on about the Meuse, sing the Guadalquivir, elect the Mississippi, and its sons-in-law, the Arkansas, the Missouri, and the Ohio, I brandish the Congo, the only river that saps your concentration, the only river that fakes tuberculosis, the only river that dances the tango and salsa and bolero and flamenco and the cha-cha-cha, the only river that thumbs its nose at you, the only river that eats meat, the only river that offs itself in the ocean, legs together, arms crossed…
I'll give you my hand to cut off, my neck to wring, my body to castrate, if what I say isn't true. In any case, I'm already castrated, and a sad sack like the Limpopo in its spare hours. In any case, what do I have to fear? Forced masturbation, the kiambi test, or murder disguised as drowning in the waters of this very river?

SOLITUDE 101

je pense à Tshela Mesu
l'avant-dernière chèvre
de ma grand-mère Julienne-mua-Mwanza
je pense à Tshela Mesu et je pleure
ah, Tshela, quelle nostalgie !

SOLITUDE 101

I think of Tshela Mesu
my grandmother Julienne mua Mwanza's
next to last goat
I think of Tshela Mesu and weep
ah Tshela, ah homesickness!

SOLITUDE 83

je veux devenir un fleuve, un long fleuve sans préface ni épilogue, juste pour emporter dans ma suite mes linges sales, un fleuve qui se jettera une fois pour toute dans l'océan sans faire des mioches par ci, des mioches par là…

SOLITUDE 83

I want to become a river, a meandering river without preface or epilogue, if only to tug my soiled linens in my current, a river that flings itself once and forever into the ocean, without siring kids along the way…

KHAL TORABULLY

Cargo Hold of Stars
COOLITUDE

TRANSLATED BY NANCY NAOMI CARLSON

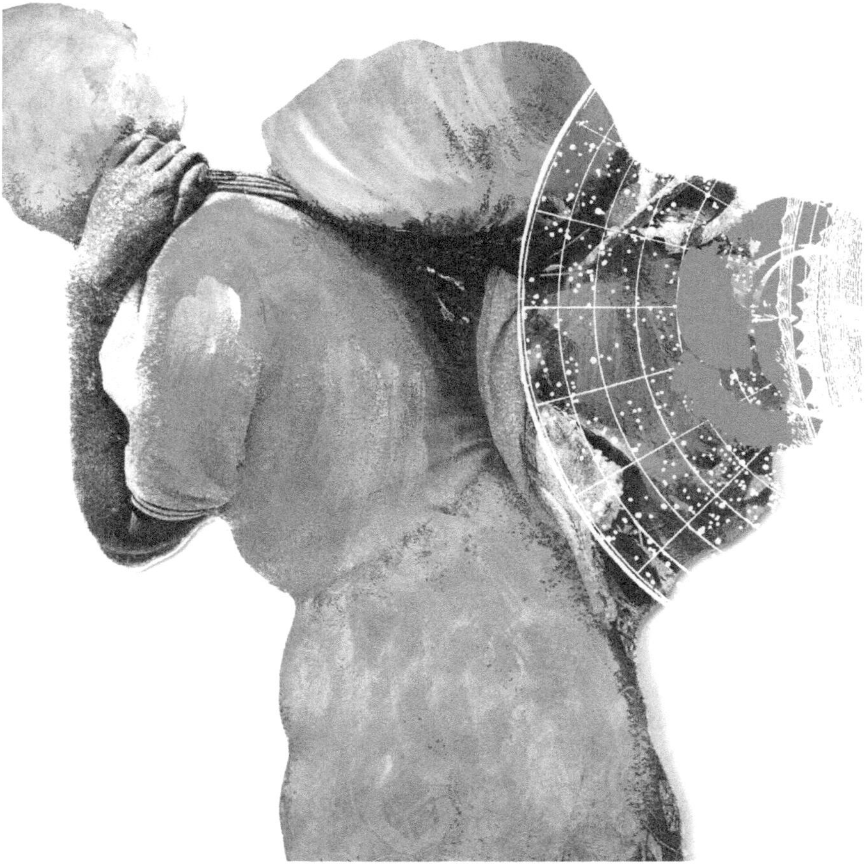

Cargo Hold of Stars: Coolitude
By Khal Torabully
Translated by Nancy Naomi Carlson

Khal Torabully, from Mauritius, is a critically acclaimed poet, essayist, film director and semiologist who has made it his life's work to give voice to the hundreds of thousands of indentured workers forced to endure horrendous conditions between the years 1849 and 1923. Indentured workers were brought mainly from China and India to the immigration depot in Port Louis where some either stayed in Mauritius as a cheap source of labour after slavery was abolished, or were sent overseas to the colonies to work the sugar cane fields. Many died on terrible sea voyages where they were packed in close quarters in the ship's cargo hold. Others died or endured harsh conditions in the colonies, where they were thrown in jail for the slightest offence, or were forced into longer periods of indenture.

Torabully has coined the term 'coolitude' from the previously pejorative term 'coolie' in a way that resembles Aimé Césaire's coining the term 'negritude'. However, the poetry of coolitude is clearly dialogical in spirit and develops an inclusive vision of peoples, memories and histories of the colonial rim and distances itself from any essentialist inspiration. It is open to the humanities and differences that are articulated in a common oceanic song, beyond the *kala pani* ('black water') taboo.

Torabully argues that indentured workers, through their rich intercultural exchanges, developed a new identity and language greater than the sum of their parts – a strong and resilient identity worthy of dignity and pride.

The original French text of *Cargo Hold of Stars: Coolitude* (*Cale d'étoiles: Coolitude*) was awarded the Prix Jean Fanchette in 1993. In this ode to the forgotten voyage of a forgotten people, Torabully has developed a 'poetics of coolitude' or 'corallian poetics' that articulates cultural diversities and biodiversities through a variegated approach to indenture or coolie trade, necessitated by his conviction that ordinary language was not equipped to bring to life the myriad diverse voices of indenture. He has created a new French, peppered with Mauritian Creole, old Scandinavian, old French, mariners' language, Indi, Bhojpuri, Urdu and neologisms. The playfulness of his language serves to underscore his deeply serious – even tragic – themes. Even the word 'cale' ('ship's cargo hold') in the French title of this book – *Cale d'étoiles* – is wordplay for the author's name, 'Khal', pronounced the same way.

Of the more than 25 books written by Torabully, including the one commissioned by the Aapravasi Ghat Trust Fund, and put on permanent display in 2013 at this UNESCO-designated world heritage site, *Cargo Hold of Stars: Coolitude* is his first book to introduce the concept of 'coolitude'. This publication represents the first time this book has appeared in English.

Nancy Naomi Carlson, from the book's introduction

Cale d'Etoiles: Coolitude [Extrait]

Je ne reconnais aux cartographes
que ma destination inconnue
mais pas les étoiles pas la chair nue
car mes vertèbres n'ont pas vu la lumière.

Je ne reconnais aux sextants
que ma chair désocéanée du temps
mais pas les vagues pas le vent sec,
car ma bouche mange la mer par son ventre bleu.
L'éclair est un bout de ciel brûlé.
Ecoutez-moi debout.
Les chiens et les chats
enfoncent l'oubli sous les pavés bleus.
N'oubliez pas, mon île,
que le premier pigeon sur ma fenêtre
avait peur de s'envoler dans vos yeux,
de peur d'y trouver une cage

From *Cargo Hold of Stars: Coolitude*

I owe the cartographers
only my unknown journey's end
but not the stars or naked flesh,
for my vertebrae never saw the light.

I owe the sextants
only my flesh, de-oceanized of time
but not the waves or the dry wind,
for my mouth consumes the sea through its blue womb.
Lightning is a bit of burnt sky.
Better listen to me, standing my ground.
Dogs and cats
bury forgetting deep under blue paving stones.
Don't forget, island of mine,
that the first pigeon perched on my windowsill
was afraid to take wing in your eyes,
for fear of finding a cage inside.

Un cœur altéré par le pays autre
sait que le ciel n'est pas immobile
que l'azur n'est sans mouvement
que pour attendre les étoiles.

Imiter les anges exige geste imperceptible

A heart altered by alien land
knows that the sky doesn't stand still
and the azure is only fixed
to await the stars.

To imitate angels takes the slightest of shifts.

Le langage m'a coolie
pour conception, mot de ma salive
coulé pur coulé sale cou lié

L'eau pure ignore les sangs
Coulé calé calqué :
deviner mes prochains itinéraires
est ma vraie moisson d'images de mer.

Ma prompte parole était si sensible
que le patois créole brûla mes fibres :
je mélangeai ma gorge au cri muet
des hommes de mer écaffés par le fouet

Language has coolied me
for conception, word of my spit:
pure cascade mixed cascade casket-bound.

Pure water pays no attention to bloodlines.
Cast clasped cloned:
guessing at what my next routes will be
is my true harvest of maritime dreams.

So sensitive were my welling words
that the Creole patois burned
my fibres: I lent my throat to the mute cry
of seamen torn apart by the whip.

Mon peuple nu, sans peau,
transfuge de lumière !
Et ma légende perdue
transfigure l'îlot d'étoiles.
Le pain rond pain fendu
évoque ma seule maison.
Béribéri
je said péripéties :
mémoire sans issue
est mon chemin de sable.

My naked people, free of skin,
transplants of light!
And my lost legend
transfigures the island of stars.
Round bread slit bread
evokes my only home.
Beriberi
I know odysseys:
memory with no escape
is my path of sand.

Ohé, je serai référent d'hommes
je partagerai la plupart.
Ohé, je réparerai fourmillement d'être
en tapant sur mon âme.
J'aurai toute sensation de pogroms,
avatar de tous les chromosomes,
ma lumière mon tawa brûlant.

La lune sème coraux blancs,
mâture dégarnie déchargée d'ombres
Ohé
les vagues sont involontaires
dans mes yeux.
Ohé
Ma seule patrie sera cri d'homme !
A chaque blessure d'homme, j'entendrai ma race !
Ohé, ohé, ohé !

Ahoy, I will be a referent of men
I will stand with the lot of them.
Ahoy, I will tend to the tingling of being
by tapping on my soul.
I'll take on all feelings of pogroms,
avatar of all chromosomes,
my light my burning *tawa*.

The moon sows white corals,
emptied masts relieved of shadows.
Ahoy
the waves are involuntary
in my eyes.
Ahoy.
My only homeland will be a human cry!
In each human wound, I will hear my race!
Ahoy, ahoy, ahoy!

La mer fut-elle
en dehors des sables
je la rattrape
l'écume fut-elle
plus rapide
que la nuée,
je la ceins
aux plus sabots d'or
du soleil.
La lumière
fut-elle
ghazal
ou mantra
je l'amasse.
La mer, Mahabaratha !

If the sea
were cut off from the sands
I'd get it back.
If ocean foam
were faster than clouds,
I'd embrace it
on the sweet golden hooves
of the sun.
If the light were
ghazal
or mantra
I'd hoard it all.
The sea, Mahabharata!

L'eau n'a pas de rives dans mes rêves
Et l'ange derrière les vagues
brandit un miroir bleu
pour défigurer les matelots.

No shore for water's drift in my dreams.
And the angel riding the backs of waves
wields a blue mirror
disfiguring faces of sailors on board.

Sur la varangue ma langue cherche une mangue
petite lune sur mât de hune me harangue :
- Raconte ma traversée coulissante
O coolie palan poulie
dis lumière pour vérité.

Sur la varangue la mangue sous ma langue
je manque à l'appel (mon cœur tangue)
comment guider le gouvernail
et donner ta chair à toute rive, à dérive, à tes rêves.
O coolie palan coolie.

Réduisez la voilure cassez le vent
de mémoire effilochée par cœur arraché
je connais ce chant je connais l'odyssée
O coolie palan colis.

On the *varangue* my tongue seeks a mango
and I'm harangued by a small topmast moon:
'Tell the tale of my curried crossing.'
O capstan pulley coolie
say light for truth.

On the *varangue*, mango under my tongue
I miss roll call (my heart reels)
how to steer the rudder
and give your flesh to all shores, all drifts, to your dreams.
O coolie capstan coolie.

Reef the sails, break the wind
of memories frayed by uprooted hearts—
I know this song, I know the odyssey.
O crating capstan coolie.

Par mon âme titubante
je connais l'origine du ciel
jusqu'à racine-la-lumière
décors des flammes toujours
mouilleront mes porcelaines.

Toute cicatrice est aube claire
même la chair même la mer

Pour les chairs incassables
mes plaies ne reviendront plus
dans mon sang hormis l'océan.

Je ne suis pas cristal
de la Compagnie des Indes
Je suis pollen d'humain
prêt à redire les cyclones
dans la chape des paroles.

Mes emblèmes sont matrices et tambours
mon fanal a charge du jour

Et mon éternité commença
aux amarres du tout premier marin
à son superbe voyage d'azur :
l'indicible dire, et tout est à dire.
Je suis pollen d'humain
accroché au gouvernail des mers.

Je suis à dire chair pure chair
chair par chair ?

With my tottering soul
I came to know how the sky began
as far back as its root-the-light.
Fiery designs
will always lick my porcelain.

Each scar is a clear dawn:
even flesh, even the sea.

For all unbreakable bodies
my wounds will no longer return
to my blood, save for the ocean's waves.

I am not crystal
from the East India Trading Company.
I am human pollen
ready to tell of the cyclones again
in the screed of words.

My emblems are wombs and drums.
My beacon is in charge of the light of day.

And my eternity began
at the mooring lines of the very first sailor
on his glorious azure crossing:
not-to-be-uttered words, and all must be told.
I am human pollen
hitched to the helm of the sea.

I am, in truth, flesh fresh flesh
flesh flush with flesh?

Pour ses premières racines
comme des rois inconnus
coolie naquit sous un multipliant :
son tatouage est ma seule marque d'oubli
ultime vésanie, mon ultime habit.

For his feeler roots
like anonymous kings
Coolie was born beneath a banyan tree:
his tattoo is my only trace of forgetting—
my supreme delirium, my supreme attire.

About the poets

SALIM BARAKAT is a Kurdish-Syrian writer who is considered one of the most innovative poets and novelists writing in the Arabic language. He was brought up in Qamishli in northern Syria and spent most of his youth there. After living in Beirut and Cyprus, he moved to Sweden in 1999, where he still resides. A prolific writer, Barakat has published dozens of novels and collections of poetry, and is distinguished from his contemporaries for the innovative use of style and theme within his writing.

* * *

NAJWAN DARWISH (b. 1978) is one of the foremost contemporary Arab poets. Since the publication of his first collection in 2000, his poetry has been hailed across the Arab world and beyond as a singular expression of the Palestinian struggle. He has published eight books in Arabic, and his work has been translated into more than 20 languages. NYRB Poets published Darwish's *Nothing More to Lose*, translated by Kareem James Abu-Zeid, in 2014, which was picked as one of the best books of the year by NPR and nominated for several awards. Darwish lives between Haifa and his birthplace, Jerusalem.

* * *

GLORIA GERVITZ (1943–2022) was a poet and translator born in Mexico City into an Eastern European Jewish immigrant family. She was awarded the Pablo Neruda Prize for Poetry in 2019. Her main body of work is Migraciones, a single poem that evolved organically over 44 years. Gervitz translated works of poetry by Samuel Beckett, Kenneth Rexroth, Lorine Niedecker, Susan Howe, and Rita Dove into Spanish.

* * *

LEE HYEMI (b. 1988) is the author of three poetry collections and an essay collection. At eighteen, she was one of the youngest winners of the JoongAng Literary Newcomer's Prize. *Unexpected Vanilla*, her second collection, was shortlisted for the 2021 National Translation Award in Poetry.

* * *

FISTON MWANZA MUJILA's writing foregrounds its debt to jazz, responds to political turbulence in his native country and its effects on everyday life, and displays an often incandescent, improvisatory verbal energy, replete with bouts of irreverent humor and surprising tonal shifts. He is the recipient of many literary prizes, including, most recently, the Peter-Rosegger-Literaturpreis (Austria, 2018). He is the author of *Tram 83*, published in English by Deep Vellum in the USA and Jacaranda Books in the UK; winner of the German International Literature Award and long-listed for the International Man Booker Prize and the Prix du Monde. Mujila was born in 1981 in Lubumbashi, Democratic Republic of Congo, and now lives in Graz, Austria.

* * *

KHAL TORABULLY is a Mauritian poet, essayist, film director and semiologist who has authored over 25 books. Aimé Césaire, the great poet from Martinique, praised Torabully's work for 'containing all of my humanity'.

About the translators

KAREEM JAMES ABU-ZEID is a translator, editor, writer, and scholar who works across multiple languages. Abu-Zeid has received numerous awards, fellowships, honors, and residencies for his work as a translator from Arabic and as a scholar, including the PEN Center USA 2017 Translation Prize and a 2018 National Endowment for the Arts translation grant. He is also the author of the forthcoming book *The Poetics of Adonis and Yves Bonnefoy: Poetry as Spiritual Practice*. He lives in the countryside just outside of Santa Fe, New Mexico.

* * *

NANCY NAOMI CARLSON is a poet, translator, and editor based in Maryland. A recipient of a literature translation fellowship from the National Endowment for the Arts, she is also a senior translation editor for *Tupelo Quarterly*.

* * *

HUDA J. FAKHREDDINE is associate professor of Arabic literature at the University of Pennsylvania. She is a translator of Arabic poetry and the author of several scholarly books.

* * *

JAYSON IWEN is the author of *Six Trips in Two Directions*, *A Momentary Jokebook*, *Gnarly Wounds*, and *Roze & Blud*, which won the 2020 Miller Williams Poetry Prize. He is a professor of writing and English literature at the University of Wisconsin–Superior.

* * *

J. BRET MANEY is a literary critic and translator from the French and Spanish. He is a recipient of several awards, including the 2020 Gulf Coast Translation Prize for his translations of Fiston Mwanza Mujila's poetry and an International Latino Book Award and PEN/Heim Translation Fund Grant for his translation of Guillermo Cotto-Thorner's novel, *Manhattan Tropics* (Arte Público, 2019), which he also co-edited. He is Assistant Professor of English at Lehman College, City University of New York.

* * *

MARK SCHAFER is a literary translator, a visual artist, and a senior lecturer at the University of Massachusetts Boston, where he teaches Spanish. He has translated works by authors from around the Spanish-speaking world, including David Huerta, Belén Gopegui, Virgilio Piñera, and Alberto Ruy Sánchez. Schafer is a founding member of the Boston Area Literary Translators Group. He lives in Roxbury, Massachusetts, the traditional and unceded territory of the Massachusett and Wampanoag Peoples.

* * *

SOJE is the translator of Lee Hyemi's *Unexpected Vanilla* (Tilted Axis Press, 2020), Lee Soho's *Catcalling* (Open Letter Books, 2021), and Choi Jin-young's *To the Warm Horizon* (Honford Star, 2021). They also make *chogwa*, a quarterly e-zine featuring one Korean poem and multiple English translations.

About the publishers

DEEP VELLUM was founded in 2013 with the mission to bring books, writers, and translators to Dallas by publishing the world's best and most diverse literature from around the world and to create a community space for all things literary. In its first 5 years Deep Vellum published 90 works in translation by international writers and hosted dozens of literary events for Dallas residents.

Deep Vellum has since expanded its operations to encompass 5 distinct publishing imprints, encompassing fiction, poetry, non-fiction, photography, translated literature and English-original books with a special focus on Dallas writers. As of 2020, approximately half of their published books are international works and half are English-original material.

* * *

NEW YORK REVIEW BOOKS brings together some of the finest writing in science, philosophy, history, politics, the arts, and literature from the *New York Review of Book*'s contributors along with new fiction and nonfiction from literary and artistic mavericks such as Amit Chaudhuri, Jonathan Buckley, and Celia Paul.

The NYRB Poets series focuses on the most vital, various, and universal form of literature: poetry. Featuring the work of poets from around the world, classical and modern, ancient and contemporary, in elegant, pocket-size editions, the series demonstrates the countless different shapes that poetry can assume, from simplest song to lyrical essay to visual image to scientific treatise, among much else. Poetry explores the boundaries of feeling, knowledge, and expression like no other art. NYRB Poets offers an unparalleled opportunity for readers to explore poetry's limitless possibilities, through collections by outstanding poets such as Pierre Reverdy, Alexander Vvedensky, Sakutarō Hagiwara, Walt Whitman, Elizabeth Willis, Najwan Darwish, Guillaume Apollinaire, Raúl Zurita, Silvina Ocampo, Arvind Krishna Mehrotra, and Denise Riley.

* * *

SEAGULL BOOKS was founded by Naveen Kishore in 1982 as an independent Indian publishing house specializing in serious books on art, theatre and cinema. It published plays by major Indian playwrights, monographs and essays by leading

Indian artists, filmscripts from the best-known Indian and European filmmakers, along with academic titles on culture, society and the various arts.

Since 2005, Seagull Books London Limited has ventured into newer fields of publishing, including English translations of fiction and non-fiction by major African, European, Asian and Latin American writers. Beginning with authors such as Guillaume Apollinaire, Jean-Paul Sartre, Roland Barthes, Jorge Luis Borges, Theodor W. Adorno, Aimé Césaire, Thomas Bernhard, Edward Said, André Gorz, Satyajit Ray, Peter Weiss and Max Frisch, Seagull Books now represents major contemporary writers such as Yves Bonnefoy, Philippe Jaccottet, Hans Magnus Enzensberger, Mahasweta Devi, Peter Handke, Pascal Quignard, Hélène Cixous, Gayatri Chakravorty Spivak, Sibylle Lewitscharoff, Marc Augé and many more. Its hallmark 'Africa List' presents writers such as Ngugi wa Thiong'o, Maryse Condé, Ivan Vladislavić, William Kentridge, Kossi Efoui and Abdourrahman A. Waberi.

* * *

TILTED AXIS PRESS is a non-profit press publishing mainly work by Asian writers, translated into a variety of Englishes.

Founded in 2015, Tilted Axis Press is based in the UK, a state whose former and current imperialism severely impacts writers in the majority world. This position, and those of its individual members, informs its practice, which is also an ongoing exploration into alternatives – to the hierarchisation of certain languages and forms, including forms of translation; to the monoculture of globalisation; to cultural, narrative, and visual stereotypes; to the commercialisation and celebrification of literature and literary translation.

About the Poetry Translation Centre

Set up in 2004, the Poetry Translation Centre is the only UK organisation dedicated to translating, publishing and promoting contemporary poetry from Africa, Asia and Latin America. We introduce extraordinary poets from around the world to new audiences through books, online resources and bilingual events. We champion diversity and representation in the arts, and forge enduring relations with diaspora communities in the UK. We explore the craft of translation through our long-running programme of workshops which are open to all.

The Poetry Translation Centre is based in London and is an Arts Council National Portfolio Organisation. To find out more about us, including how you can support our work, please visit: www.poetrytranslation.org.

About the Sarah Maguire Prize

The Sarah Maguire Prize for Poetry in Translation has been established in the memory of Sarah Maguire (1957–2017), the founder of the Poetry Translation Centre and champion of international poetry. The aim of the prize is to showcase the most exciting contemporary poetry from around the world, and to champion the art of poetry translation.

The prize is awarded every two years for the best book of poetry from a living poet from a non-European country, in English translation, published anywhere in the world. The winning poet and their translator(s) divide a prize of £3,000.

Submissions to the 2024 edition of the prize will open in May 2023 and close in December 2023. Eligible entries must be published in 2022–2023 and submissions must be made by the publisher.

To find out more, please visit www.poetrytranslation.org/sarah-maguire-prize